RICHARD LINDNER

DORE ASHTON

RICHARD LINDNER

HARRY N. ABRAMS, INC. *PUBLISHERS* NEW YORK

Frontispiece
Plate 1. THE MEETING. 1953.
Oil on canvas, 60×72″.
The Museum of Modern Art, New York

PUBLISHED-1970.

Library of Congress Catalog Card Number: 69–12799
All rights reserved. No part of the contents of this book may be
reproduced without the written permission of the publishers
HARRY N. ABRAMS, INCORPORATED, NEW YORK
Printed and bound in Japan

CONTENTS

LIST OF PLATES

Colorplates are marked with an asterisk *

R. LINDNER

WHENEVER RICHARD LINDNER's paintings are exhibited—whether in Britain, France, Italy, or the United States—the written responses show a remarkable uniformity of diction. His paintings are called perverse, Freudian, nightmarish, obsessive, lascivious, decadent, deviant, and frequently, "German," implying a specific harshness and cruelty.

Critics have relished describing what they believe to be Lindner's erotic fantasies, and some have even gone so far as to advise him to see an analyst. They have almost without exception treated the work and the man as an indivisible unit.

On the whole, they have centered their attention on Lindner's preoccupation with women in their role as temptresses. By ascribing Lindner's visions of corseted whores and gauntleted chorus girls to his personal and aberrated imagination, these critics obscure the complexity and strong element of paradox in his work, and they neglect two important dimensions: the literary and the historical.

Lindner has always maintained that he is a literary artist. His work confirms him, while it also reveals him as critic, commentator, and, most important, a strong plastic artist. His work may spring from Freudian depths in legible symbols, but there is little benefit in adopting this exclusive interpretive point of view. Karl Jaspers warned his disciples not to try to ascribe specific features of madness to Hölderlin's first poetry after his break-

down. There is a creative force, he wrote, which cannot be analyzed into its components.

In Lindner's case, the quick identification of psychoanalytic clues adds little to, and in fact detracts from, the full measure of his achievement.

By contrast, the circumstances of Lindner's life—his Bavarian background, his flight from Germany, his decisive emigration—must be given considerable weight. The nature of his art demands attention to its sources. His concern with the spoken, or descriptive, element in art is profound. As he told his students, "If you can't paint it, write it."[1]

No one can judge to what degree events shape an artist. There is no way of determining the exact recipe for illuminating an oeuvre. Are biographical clues misleading? Can an artist slip through his epoch untouched, an Ariel without moorings? Obviously, discourse can lead anywhere and rarely leads to definitive interpretation. Still, Lindner's work abounds in significant clues concerning his past—clues that may point to an insoluble mystery, but that nevertheless cannot be ignored.

There is much literature concerning the double nature of the artist, his awareness of his two selves—the creating self and the earthbound, ordinary self. Rimbaud's "Je est un autre," Proust's response to a questioner: "C'était un autre moi qui a écrit ça," and Symons' commentary on Beardsley are particularly appropriate to Lindner: "Beardsley did not believe in his own en-

9

chantments, was never haunted by his own terrors, and, in his queer sympathy and familiarity with evil, had none of the ardours of a lost soul."

Lindner must be considered apart from his work because the nature of his discourse in paint is detached, no matter what the sources of his fantasies. Central to his entire oeuvre is the theme of the onlooker, the observer, the uninvolved spectator. He can appear either as a dreaming youth, a voyeur, a master of ceremonies, a pimp, or a fantasizing bourgeois. He is, as several titles indicate, the Stranger, the agent through whom Lindner's visions are distanced, cooled.

Lindner's way of looking at the world was deeply conditioned by the experiences of his youth, and his paintings issue from a common vocabulary that has survived from the 1920s. When he was young, for instance, it was taken for granted that circuses, variety shows, and street life were effective analogues of society, and could be manipulated symbolically by the artist.

Consider, for instance, Lindner's important character, the *Ceremoniemeister* who appears in his early paintings. The *Ceremoniemeister* was a stock figure in early twentieth-century art. He appears in Apollinaire's revolutionary play, *Les Mamelles de Tirésias*; he elucidates Wedekind's plays; he presents Brecht's *Threepenny Opera*; he appears as Manager in Satie and Picasso's *Parade*; and he persists later in Max Ophuls' *Lola Montez*, the films of Fellini, and in the literature of today with its ironic first-person accounts. The detached Master of Ceremonies, whether he arrives via Berlin nightclubs or international circuses or jazz-age cabarets, is a perennial instrument for the artist who seeks to distance his ironic commentary.

Another way of relating Lindner's work and the vocabulary of his youth which left such a deep impression is to consider his view of women, regarded as so extraordinarily perverse by so many critics.

In historical context, Lindner's representation of woman as temptress extends a tradition that was generated in the late nineteenth century and is still alive. It was common practice then among the Symbolist poets, for instance, to deal with women as Liliths, Delilahs, and Eves.

The uneasy awareness of the shifting role of women in Western society was reflected in two important writers of the late nineteenth century, both of whom Lindner read seriously during his student years.

Most familiar to him were the works of Nietzsche, and particularly *Thus Spake Zarathustra*, which he says was his first children's book. (His precocious reading habits can be gauged by his claim that when he was only six years old, he possessed a history of erotica by Edward Fuchs.) Nietzsche, for Lindner, was a man with power over women, with whom he had complex relationships. Nietzsche was physically a small man. Lindner, as a small man, was deeply curious about him. Lindner sees Nietzsche as both a victim of woman and as a powerful victimizer—an attitude clearly expressed in his paintings, which he believes Nietzsche would have liked.

The other writer whose intense feelings about women are threaded with ambivalence was Rimbaud. Lindner has stated repeatedly that what he admires in women are their secrets. "Women are more imaginative than men. They have secrets they don't even know they have." The belief that women have resources different from and richer than those of men was stated as early as 1871 by Rimbaud, who prophesied: "When the infinite servitude of woman shall have ended, when she will be able to live by and for herself; then man—hitherto abominable—having given her her freedom, she too will be a poet. Woman will discover the unknown. Will her world be different from ours? She will discover strange, unfathomable things, repulsive, delicious. We shall take them, we shall understand them."[2]

Plate 2.
THE VISITOR. 1953.
Pastel, 25 1/2 × 19 1/2″. Collection Ingeborg
Wiener-ten Haeff, New York

Here the Eve theme is treated somewhat differently, since Rimbaud recognized the unjustness of women's servitude, but basically he sees woman as the initiator, as Eve instigating action, as a creature especially suited to "strange, unfathomable things."

The twentieth-century "liberation" of sex brought further extrapolations on the Eve theme. The conventional view, which is essentially the view Lindner took when he commenced painting seriously, was that women were both victims of man's lust and amoral seductresses. This view was widely expressed in the mores, the literature, and the visual arts during Lindner's *Wanderjahre*. In addition, the early twentieth century was a period of aggressive suffragette activity in both Europe and the United States. Women emerged as political leaders— Rosa Luxembourg in Germany, for instance, and later La Pasionaria in Spain. Woman as a modern motif took on a special coloration in our century, and Lindner shared with his artistic confreres a vivid interest in her new guises.

Even the harshness, the cruelty often remarked in Lindner's paintings, cannot be seen solely as sublimation. The hard light and graphic details in the endless Early Renaissance torture and martyr scenes cannot always have been a projection of the artist's own sentiments. Such narratives were part of the lore, the attitudes of the period.

Lindner's work, like a good novel, deals expressly with the lore of his period, which he transforms, by means of wit and plastic invention, into a synthetic vision, a parable of the world not anchored in any special time or place.

To identify Lindner wholly with his cast of characters would be like identifying Nabokov with his protagonist in *Lolita*, forgetting the Nabokov who so consummately identified with Gogol, or Pushkin, or poor Pnin. It would be to forget Nabokov the grand bourgeois, whose style in literature is certainly separated by his imagination from his style in life.

THE VISITOR

Lindner began painting seriously, or at least exclusively, only in the early 1950s. He worked like a drowning man, recapitulating his experiences, reciting the facts to himself painting by painting, in order to purge himself of his past. In the course of this assiduous effort, which resulted, he feels, in his finally becoming a New Yorker, he offered a host of clues concerning his formative years.

All of his early paintings are based on facts from his past. They can be seen as a series of conjectures derived from the facts and tested by the artist for veracity. In some cases, the "facts" proved irrelevant, and Lindner dropped them in future work (for instance, his early image of the *Wunderkind*). But in other cases these memories, painted into the fantasy of his canvas, proved fundamental to Lindner's vision and were the armatures for his American structures.

One of his most compelling paintings of this early period is *The Visitor* (plate 48), a painting which in its very atmosphere conjures memory and suggests an era gone by. The visitor appears first in a fine pastel (plate 2) as a physical type straight out of Lindner's middle-class youth in Bavaria. He has the soft, well-fleshed face of the good bourgeois seeking he knows not what. He is the same bourgeois, in fact, who conjures a balmy dream of a voluptuous Bavarian servant girl in the 1953 watercolor *Man and Woman* (plate 3).

In the pastel *Visitor*, the overgrown schoolgirl in her sailor dress gazes at her visitor mildly. She is like a porcelain doll with tiny hands and head. The encounter is rather mystical, and without predatory overtones.

Plate 3.
MAN AND WOMAN. 1953.
Watercolor and pencil, 39 3/8 × 29 1/4″.
Collection Mr. and Mrs. Herman Elkon,
New York

Plate 4.
Lindner's uncle and aunt,
variety artists

In the painting, the visitor takes on a wholly different character. He is the Svengali-like *Ceremoniemeister* whose presence alone indicates the theatrical quality of the presentation. He is dressed for the role. The girl with her hoop no longer gazes in a friendly way at her visitor. She moves with trancelike steps toward him. She scarcely sees him. She is isolated in her adolescent fantasy.

Their environment is closed, and clearly alludes to theater or circus. The scarlet wall could be a dressing-room wall. There is the stillness of theater here. And, she is an actress, no longer a porcelain doll.

This visitor in his double role—as the dreaming bourgeois and the director of the spectacle—persists in Lindner's work in one guise and another. Lindner himself may be said to identify with the visitor. It is Lindner who pulls the strings to make his marionettes perform, and it is Lindner who watches.

The essentially theatrical character of Lindner's work issues from the lore of his youth as well as from his strong natural affinity for theater. Among the members of his family he remembers most fondly an uncle and an aunt who were variety artists. The uncle, Lindner recalls with pride, wrote popular songs that were heard throughout the streets in Bavaria. (This uncle, by the way, physically resembles the visitor and subsequent characters in Lindner's paintings.)

While Lindner was still a small boy, German theater was celebrated throughout the world for the vitality of its modern fare. It was a primary source of art, an important part of the lives of the community, bourgeois and bohemian alike. It was not unusual for a boy of Lindner's circumstances to frequent the theater weekly while still in his early teens.

There was an active repertory theater in Nuremberg, where Lindner first saw the then avant-garde plays of Hauptmann, Strindberg, and Wedekind, which made a profound impression on him. Probably it was Wedekind, more than any literary or visual artist in the twentieth century, who influenced Lindner. (Many artists were attracted to theater in the early part of the century. Kandinsky, Barlach, Beckmann, Kokoschka, Schlemmer, and Picasso even tried their hand at writing plays.)

Lindner has many affinities with Wedekind, even biographically. Like Wedekind, he had an American mother and, like him, he had a favorite sister who was a well-known singer. He shares his predecessor's interest in colorful, theatrical characters whom he sees, as did Wedekind, as both examples of, and outcasts from, a corrupt bourgeois society.

Wedekind was one of the first writers in Europe to use the life of the variety-theater artists as thematic material. He was apparently genuinely attracted to the rough and often sordid characters who plied their various trades in the capitals of Europe. As a young man in Munich, he befriended one Willi Rudinoff, described as an actor, acrobat, painter, and imitator of animal voices. Later, in Paris, he consorted mainly with circus folk and became a close friend of Willi Gretor, a painter, writer, swindler, and one of the most accomplished forgers of pictures of his day.

These propensities of young Wedekind's led him to the Grand Guignol and Variété theaters, where he drew

Plate 5. Lindner and his aunt, "a local beauty"

Plate 6.
Lindner with his
parents and sister

Plate 7.
Lindner, left,
with his brother

inspiration for his forthcoming plays a full decade before Picasso and Max Jacob related the sad lives of performing carnival and variety artists.

The Wedekind revival during Lindner's school years included performances of his diptych *The Earth Spirit (Der Erdgeist)* and *Pandora's Box.* Here, Wedekind uses his *Ceremoniemeister* to introduce the performance. The prologue to *The Earth Spirit* opens:

"The curtain rises to disclose the entrance to a tent from which emerges to the sound of cymbals and the beating of drums an animal tamer dressed in a vermilion red frockcoat, white tie; he has long black curly hair, white breeches and top boots; in his left hand he carries a riding whip . . ."[3]

Wedekind uses this *Ceremoniemeister* to establish his position as a stranger, a visitor, a detached onlooker. Lion Feuchtwanger explained that "Wedekind tries to take up a position outside the world he has created and from this Archimedean point of vantage, to demonstrate as a detached observer the tragic absurdity of his world and ours."[4]

In keeping with this Archimedean viewpoint, the characters in Wedekind's plays are types, not individuals. He cultivated habits of observation so that he could describe the type through the individual detail. (This emphasis on type rather than individual is found in the Expressionist plays of the immediate postwar period again and again. Georg Kaiser, one of the most prolific young playwrights—he had thirteen plays produced in 1917–18 alone—nearly always designated his characters in general terms: Billionaire, Worker, Chief Engineer, Figures in Blue, Figures in Yellow, etc.)

The types that recur throughout Lindner's work— they change decade, costume, or mask, but they remain basic types—are decidedly seen by their author as elements in a theatrical presentation. Lindner's allegories of modern existence, like Wedekind's, require the once-removed visitor, the master of ceremonies, the stranger. When the stranger appears five years later in Dick Tracy guise, he functions as does the visitor in 1953: he is an ambiguous figure, at once watching and participating. And he is also subject to the magic and dominance of woman, as we feel the visitor is. Even with his gold-headed cane, the visitor cannot combat that remote and assured gaze of the flaxen-haired, false child.

THE MEETING

A careful consideration of Lindner's first major "machine," *The Meeting* (frontispiece; plate 8), is an excellent entree into the meaning of his work. It was his first important painting both in terms of its ambition and the significance it had for his future development.

This painting, at once autobiographical and symbolic, represents to Lindner his entrance into the New World, a successfully performed rite of passage. It purged him of a past (not wholly, but enough to release his imagination), and set him in a present to which he remains totally faithful.

The Meeting is a watershed painting, and also a key, a lexicon of his basic visual vocabulary. Nearly all his favored types are represented: the wise and sensual child-woman; the *grande dame;* the legendary figure, Ludwig II; the innocent schoolboy (himself); the animal; and the woman as eternal principle. In addition, there are portraits of important contemporaries in Lindner's circle who, like him, made New York a center of existence while retaining their European culture. These people are as much Lindner's family as the sister and aunt represented in the upper registers of the painting.

The sister, at the upper left, is one of Lindner's precocious children, reminiscent of Balthus' adolescent girls.

Plate 8. Sketch for THE MEETING. 1953. Pencil, 12 1/8 × 14 1/8″. Collection the artist

In her musing expression, Lindner conveys his memory of her as one of the first women he knew with secrets. "My mother, being an American puritan, watched over her so closely that she *had* to have secrets. We lived in a Victorian epoch."

Seven years older than Lindner, the sister loomed large in his life. When, at the age of nineteen, she was already a celebrated opera singer, Lindner saw her perform in *La Traviata*. She died two years later, in 1915, of influenza. Lindner's mother made certain that this death would be of great moment in his young life by taking him and his brother to the cemetery every Sunday.

The other feminine presence in his childhood which seems to have helped form his attitude toward women is the aunt pictured beside him in the painting, wearing the very latest dress and a rather indifferent, self-sufficient expression. She was what Lindner calls "the local beauty," whose charms he early admired.

All three of the family portraits in this crowded, synoptic painting are drawn in a remote and generalizing manner, contrasting with the specific features of the friends, Evelyn Hofer, Hedda Sterne, and Saul Steinberg. Lindner shows himself gazing out, a musing schoolboy on the verge of puberty. His features—and those of his aunt and sister—are the features of the china dolls produced in his native Nuremberg. His toylike evocation of himself recalls the fact that his native city, Nuremberg, was a center of toy manufacture from the fourteenth century on, excelling in mechanical toys and clockmaking. The tin soldier originated in Nuremberg, in the eighteenth century. Nuremberg also listed the earliest registered doll makers.

Lindner's preoccupation with toys—he still collects them—may not have originated with Nuremberg, although it was certainly fed by local tradition. Rather, Lindner is like one of those children described so aptly by

Plate 9. China doll wearing a student's uniform

Baudelaire in *Morale du Joujou*:[5] "I think that generally children act on their toys, in other words, that their choice is directed by dispositions and desires—vague, it is true—not formulated but very real. Nevertheless, I would not say that the contrary doesn't occur, that is, that toys act on the child, above all in the case of literary or artistic predestination."

Plate 10. Nuremberg c. 1450. From Hartmann Schedel's WELTCHRONIK, published in Nuremberg, 1493   Plate 11. View of Nuremberg

Baudelaire considered that the toy is the first initiation of the child into art; that children demonstrate in their games a great "faculty of abstraction and high imaginative power" and that the "immense *mundus*" of the child is as easily enriched by the barbaric or primitive toy as it is by "these marvels which are more an homage to the parasitic servility to wealth of the parents than a gift to childish poetry."

Perhaps Baudelaire's most pertinent observation is on the childish need to take apart or destroy toys. "Most youngsters," he wrote, "want above all to *see the soul*. . . . I don't have the courage to reproach this as childish foolishness: it is the first metaphysical tendency."

Lindner is certainly an extension of that child who wants to take his toys apart. Quite aside from his stated admiration of the natural creativeness of children ("I have seen children and madmen at work. The craft comes if you have something to express. Everyone is creative."),

there is constant recourse in his paintings to toylike images: the brightly colored sparkler transformed into a target; the china doll; the stuffed animal; and, lately, the elaborate machines that grace the toystores of adults in Hollywood, Times Square, and Las Vegas. In *Stranger No. 2* (plate 65), for instance, we see the woman figure dissected as if she were a paper doll, with dotted lines emphasizing the impression.

Lindner's preoccupation with toys may have been inspired by Nuremberg itself, a diminutive city and, in a sense, a toylike evocation of a past that is far more vivid than the present. The town is almost wholly given to recall. It is a monument to past imaginations. When Lindner wandered in its narrow streets, he could not have missed the pervasive nostalgia and the theatrical settings for past dramas.

This fairytale city, "Trading Staple of the German World in the old days, Toyshop of the German World

20

in these new, Albert Dürer's and Hans Sachs' city," as Carlyle wrote, is densely built. From a distance one saw a pattern of red roofs, the ancient castle, and 187 antique towers. Hermann Kesten describes his hero's approach to the city in *The Twins of Nuremberg*:

"The streets grew elegant—rows of villas with marble pillared porticoes. These in turn led to a round tower complete with rampart, moat, and shady walk. And Lust stepped into the Middle Ages: there were houses with pointed gables, forsaken courtyards, winding alleys no wider than a man, each one named after an extinct handicraft, each reeking of a long-forgotten smell."[6]

The river Pegnitz, which meanders slowly through the town, is flanked with Renaissance houses as mysterious and provocative as the houses of Venice. In this narrow medieval town, a boy's imagination could soar. Its greatness was authentic. It had been the home of many distinguished artists, scientists, writers, and musicians. "I have chosen Nuremberg for my place of residence because there I find without difficulty all the peculiar instruments necessary for astronomy," wrote Johannes Muller in 1471, "and there it is easiest for me to keep in touch with the learned of all countries, for Nuremberg, thanks to the perpetual journeyings of her merchants, may be counted as the center of Europe."[7]

By the time Lindner was born, Nuremberg was a museum of past brilliance, and he often says he was reared in the wrong town. It was no European center, although tourists flocked to see its quaint beer halls, Dürer's house, and what was left of its treasures. (Nuremberg shamelessly sold off its masterpieces during the last century. There are relatively few works of Dürer, Wolgemut, Vischer, Stoss, and Krafft in her collections.)

They also flocked to see the famous Iron Maiden, a torture instrument of great ingenuity. Prisoners were condemned to *die verfluchte Jungfer*—to kiss the maiden,

and in her embrace feel a thousand spikes slowly sink into their flesh. Critics have been quick to link Lindner's occasionally cruel, mechanical images with early impressions of the Iron Maiden. But that would be like linking Hogarth with the torture instruments in London Tower; Tintoretto with the even more elaborate Venetian instruments; Raphael with the Roman specialties, and so on.

Rather, the Nuremberg influence on Lindner was probably oblique, and certainly something to react against. But the place itself and its confined spaces no doubt made their impression. In a banal travel book, an author mentions that "the extraordinary color scheme sometimes makes everything look like children's toys or a stage setting."[8]

If this diminutive toy city had its impact on Lindner's imagination, the other side of Nuremberg's life in the twentieth century might well have registered in his subconscious. Nuremberg had a bleak industrial quarter, crowded with poor and ugly working-class dwellings. It had grime, grayness, and all the squalid activities that impoverished factory workers undertook to mask their miseries.

When the Inflation wracked Germany after World War I, Nuremberg's poor took to the streets and must have looked very like the poor of Berlin depicted by George Grosz. This netherworld of Nurembergers made up the pool of the disinherited that rallied to the Hitler flag a few years later. Many were eventually condemned in their own town during the Nuremberg trials.

Certainly the darker and less picturesque side of Nuremberg remained with Lindner, as it remained with several of his friends who also emigrated to the United States. A kind of hate-love and a strong attraction to the sweeter flavors of Bavarian life bound together such artists as René Bouché, Ilse Getz, and Lindner. Although their native town was a source of tragedy in their personal lives, these artists never quite purged themselves of its charms.

Lindner lived a bourgeois childhood, cosy in the ways of German society before World War I. Dreadful and foreboding events swept through Europe in his childhood and youth, but he does not seem to have been deeply aware of them or shaken by them until his maturity. His malaise is retrospective.

Looking back, he can see that there was a certain aimlessness in his patterns as an adolescent which could have been the result of the tremendous confusion attending World War I and its aftermath. He was a student in the Nuremberg Conservatory, preparing for his brief career as a concert pianist (he gave only two public recitals), when Germany was defeated. The hectic disorganization that rent the fabric of Nuremberg society did not affect him directly, but it did make his studies and the idea of planning his future seem futile.

"Actually, I played the piano because there was no future," he recalls, and adds that he became an art student for the same reason. "This was the first period after a Victorian epoch. The first time all the security was gone. I was born in a time when one had to become an artist, or a criminal."

The big city, to which Lindner went when he was in his early twenties, was Munich, the center of Bavarian culture. Lindner often mentions his Bavarian background, and his intimate friends point out that he is characteristically Bavarian, qualifying it by saying he still speaks with a Bavarian accent; he is, as one friend says, "strong with a great peasant quality; straightforward, not Anglicized and good-mannered like the Northerners." Another friend mentions the minor fact that Lindner, like his compatriots, is still a beer drinker and a pipe smoker; that he is, like the Bavarians, full of self-mockery but not irony.

The Bavarians are well fed (as we see in *The Meeting*) and jovial. The idea of *Gemütlichkeit* is deeply ingrained. Something in the cloistral space of *The Meeting*—as in several early paintings with their confined cubicles containing larger-than-life figures—evokes the heavy-beamed, low-ceilinged, stuffy, and *gemütlich* atmosphere of Bavaria.

A number of significant twentieth-century writers have tried to define the character of Bavaria and, as a record of what Lindner felt he had to purge, their descriptions are valuable. While Lindner was still an infant, Wedekind returned to Munich because of "the frenzy of mute saturnalia in the air." The carnival spirit of Munich, about which all writers remark, is discussed by Feuchtwanger in *Success*.[9] Speaking of an entrepreneur's plans to open cabarets in Munich, during the very years when Lindner was a student there, Feuchtwanger writes:

"He was moved by the instinct for the decorative, for the theatrical, which at intervals had always emerged in the people of the Bavarian upland . . . the popular fetes of Munich in which he had taken part as a boy with such emotion, the regular yearly fairs in the public meadows, popular carnivals accompanied by an ear-splitting din, the Wagner festivals, the military parades, the magnificent procession on the day of Corpus Christi, the carnival balls in the German Theater, the tumultuous beer orgies in the gigantic halls of the great breweries. . . ."

Life, then, was pointedly jolly as the Munich song goes: "As long as the Isar runs green through the town / You'll find jolly good fellows in Munich."

But there were undertones. In the brooding descriptions of medieval towns with their dark brown atmosphere in Thomas Mann's *Doctor Faustus*, the sources of future Bavarian crimes emerge.[10] Mann's aloofness lends his analysis of Bavarian mores all the more weight.

It is easy to understand Lindner's deep respect for Mann, whom he remembers from the first days of his exile as a grave, composed, and impressive figure, somewhat remote from his contemporaries. Lindner's love of secrets was probably roused by Mann's taciturn presence. The semblance of detachment in Mann's measured prose is very congenial to Lindner, who strives in his own pictorial language to maintain a similar sober distance from the emotionally powerful materials he utilizes. Mann describes first the Munich of before World War I—the Bavarian atmosphere in which Lindner spent his first thirteen years. He speaks of "the self-indulgent comfort of its ways, the suggestion it had of all-the-year-round carnival freedom," of its atmosphere, "a little mad and quite harmless," and calls it a self-satisfied Capua.

The Munich of the late Regency, Mann says, was full of art shops and palaces of decorative crafts, of monster fairs and "lusty folkishness." It had esoteric coteries "performing the aesthetic devotion behind the Siegestor; its Bohemia, well bedded-down in public approval and fundamentally easygoing."

World War I, however, "put an end forever to the idyl of guilelessness in the city on the Isar and its Dionysiac easy goingness. . . . "

Still, from Lindner's reminiscences of his youth in Munich after the end of the idyl, it would seem that many of the old habits survived. The taste for costumes, masks, and theatrical dress-up in his paintings may be partly credited to the mores of Bavaria in his youth. Possibly the erotic allegories of one of Munich's celebrated professors, Franz von Stuck, also helped to focus his interests. Stuck, who had been the unsatisfactory teacher of Kandinsky and Klee, was highly regarded by the Munich bourgeoisie and his work was widely exhibited. His cold precision in rendering elaborate allegories which often verged on pornography appealed

Plate 12. Franz von Stuck. THE SIN. Oil on canvas, 37 3/8 × 23 5/8". Bayerische Staatsgemäldesammlungen, Munich

23

Kameraden!
Willkommen in der Heimat!

Ein erneuertes, verjüngtes Deutschland begrüßt Euch.
Das morsche System des Militarismus ist zusammengebrochen.
Die veraltete Kastenregierung ist weggefegt für immer.

Als
freie Männer
betretet Ihr den heiligen Boden eines
freien Deutschlands!
Nehmt den ersten Gruß des neuen Vaterlandes an seine tapferen Söhne!
Dank für Eure Taten! Dank für Eure Ausdauer!
Hört zugleich die Stimme der Heimat!

Sorgt alle dafür, daß das freie Deutschland nicht
abermals geknechtet werde!
Tod der Anarchie! Tod dem Chaos!

Haltet Ordnung!
Sichert den ruhigen Verlauf der Demobilisation!
An ihr hängt alles!

Nur durch Ordnung erhalten wir
Freiheit, Frieden und Brot
Seid willkommen!

Plate 13.
Poster circulated by
the Social Democratic Party
in 1918

Plates 14, 15, 16. Three portraits of Ludwig II of Bavaria, showing him at various stages during his lifetime

to them in the same way, probably, that Lindner appeals to them. Lindner remembers being tremendously impressed by one of Stuck's most celebrated paintings, *The Sin* (plate 12), which, he says, prevented him from ever using a snake in his pictures.

The solidly Bavarian easygoingness can be detected in Lindner when he speaks of the chaotic events immediately after the War. For instance, when revolution broke out in Bavaria and Kurt Eisner, a left-wing socialist, became chief of the new state, Lindner recalls only that members of his family who were officers tried not to go out in the streets—they had only their uniforms— and tore off the insignia of their rank. Of Eisner, who was

assassinated by the proto-Nazi Freikorps, he recalls: "I met him once. A nice professor type. He refused to have protection, saying that if they wanted to shoot him, then he oughtn't to be a leader. He had a very long beard, like out of a Chaplin movie."

The 1918 revolution seemed to him mild, and the king was an acceptable figure, a "man of the people who had a milk farm, and who used to pose at the Academy." The Bavarians, Lindner says, hated only the Prussians, and could never have made a real revolution.

Like most middle-class Bavarians, Lindner seemed only dimly aware of the cataclysmic signs around him. The poster (plate 13) circulated after the 1918 ceasefire by the Social Democrats, whom Lindner was soon to join officially, would probably have seemed natural to him despite its anomalies. It proclaims that the system of rotten militarism has broken down, and that the outdated caste regime has been swept away forever. It proudly welcomes German soldiers back to a free Fatherland and then, in commanding tones, it exhorts them to KEEP ORDER! Only through order, it insists, will freedom, peace, and bread be obtained.

To admire order, as Lindner probably did unreflectingly, was not to ignore that other Bavarian tradition of caustic criticism reflected in the columns of *Simplicissimus*. Founded in 1896, this famous illustrated weekly vehemently satirized the officer class, the overfed bourgeoisie, the Kaiser, and, toward the end of its life, Hitler. It had a staff of exceptionally gifted caricaturists, many of whom Lindner knew well in the late 1920s, among them T. T. Heine. The tradition of critical illustration so powerfully fostered in *Simplicissimus* may well have influenced Lindner.

It was, however, the slow, comfortable, cosy, orderly, and only mildly perverse Bavaria that Lindner describes in the upper registers of *The Meeting*. Not the sophisticated Bavaria as represented by the bohemians in Munich's artists' district, Schwabing, or in the cafés and cabarets where the master of ceremonies introduced clever skits, political satires, and songs. And where, incidentally, the tables were connected by telephone, making all kinds of perverse delights and adventures possible. (The telephone as an instrument of erotic longing still appears regularly in Lindner's paintings.)

In Lindner's unsophisticated Bavaria, the hero is not a Kurt Eisner, or T. T. Heine, or Karl Kraus, or the Kaiser, but the legendary King Ludwig II (plates 14, 15), who has preoccupied Lindner since his childhood.

King Ludwig, in his anachronistic costume, his handsome face beginning to take on the unhealthy flesh of his later years (plate 16), is a very important figure in *The Meeting*, and is depicted at least twice more in Lindner's works. This is surely one of Lindner's obsessions, but it is, as he says, the fantasy of all of Bavaria. He grew up with the legend of Ludwig. All of Bavaria—at least peasant Bavaria—embellished this fantasy. "He was a fairytale king who was glorified by his beauty," Lindner says. "To this day Bavarian peasants carry his photographs."

Again, commentators have erred in imagining that Ludwig, with all his eccentricities and his insane extravagances, is a peculiar obsession of Lindner's. Lindner shared with many sensitive artists of his time a curiosity about the mad monarch and a willingness to consider the madness as genius.

No more sober judge exists than Thomas Mann, and yet he stages a heated argument about the mad king in *Doctor Faustus*. He briefly recapitulates the story of Ludwig's youth, his poetic beauty, his misanthropy, his later homosexuality, and his passion for building. His protagonists argue about Ludwig's death: how he was certified insane by doctors who never examined him, and how he drowned, taking his doctor-keeper with him. The certification, one of Mann's characters argues heatedly, was a "brutal piece of philistinism, and in addition a political move in the interest of succession." He pursues the argument, one suspects, as Mann himself would have, against Rudi, who "took his stand on the interpretation, not so much popular as bourgeois and official, that the King was 'completely crackers.'":

"A sovereign king, surrounded by devotion, dispensed from criticism and responsibility, licensed, in support of his dignity, to live in a style forbidden to the wealthiest private man, could give way to such fantastic tastes and tendencies; to the gratification of such baffling passions and desires, such nervous attractions and repulsions, that a haughty and consummate exploitation of them might very easily look like madness. . . . These castles, certainly, were monuments of royal misanthropy."

Mann indignantly refers to the six alienists who had condemned him without ever having spoken a word to him. "A conversation with him about music and poetry would just as well have convinced these idiots of his madness. . . ."

When the peasants had seen Ludwig driving through his mountains at night, alone, wrapped in furs, in a golden sledge with outriders, in the gleam of torches, the narrator asserts, "they had seen no madman, but a king after their own rude romantic hearts."

The persistence of this legend is noted by Feuchtwanger writing of the early 1930s in Bavaria: "The well-beloved King Ludwig II, this rumor ran, was still alive. This King Ludwig, filled with a Caesarian consciousness of power, had identified himself with Louis XIV of France, had built extravagant and pompous castles in almost inaccessible positions, had fostered like a new Maecenas obsolete artistic details, had kept like a new Pharaoh his distance from the people, and precisely through this had excited their enthusiastic love. When he died at last, the people refused to believe it. . . ."[11]

In the peasant cottages described by Feuchtwanger, "the giant image of the second Ludwig with his rosy face, his black moustache, his curls, his blue eyes, lived on in the fantasy of the people. Countless portraits of the King in purple and ermine, in blazing uniform, in silver mail standing in a boat drawn by swans, hung in rooms of peasants and respectable townspeople."

With his keen eye, his journalist's eye, Lindner paints a Ludwig very like the Ludwig Feuchtwanger describes.

The Ludwig who attracted Lindner was not only the Ludwig of the mad castles, but the genuine patron of the arts who made Wagner's life bearable and brought to fruition Wagner's dreams. It was the Ludwig whom

Plate 17. Neuschwanstein castle, built by Ludwig II of Bavaria

Mark Twain tartly reproduced in 1878, writing: "The King of Bavaria is a poet and has a poet's eccentricities with the advantage over all other poets of being able to gratify them no matter what form they take."[12] Twain was speaking about the command performances at which Ludwig was often the only spectator, and about which the gossip in Munich was greatly embellished. No doubt Twain had heard all about the strange performances in the beer halls he visited.

Then there is the aspect of Ludwig that must evoke a

sympathy in Lindner: Ludwig's great love of theater, his prolonged childhood in which he manufactures increasingly elaborate settings and acquires stranger and stranger toys.

Brought up in Hohenschwangau, a towering castle in the Bavarian Alps surrounded by fir forests, Ludwig was exposed constantly to the world of legend. It was here that Lohengrin performed his feats. Scenes of the legend of the Swan Knight were all over the castle, and there were swans on the lake.

When the slender prince became king, he built an artificial lake on the third floor of the royal residence which he stocked with swanlike gondolas, and on which he floated in the costume of the Swan Knight.

His next venture was a castle dedicated to the Nibelungen, high above Hohenschwangau, which he called Neuschwanstein (plate 17). Here he indulged a feudal fantasy, building battlements, watchtowers, and drawbridges as settings for his Wagnerian fantasies.

Tiring of the Swan Knight role, Ludwig became a passionate student of Louis XIV, with whom he ultimately identified completely. The result was Linderhof, his very own Versailles. The guide book reads: "Inspired by the Trianon, the florid Rococo palace is gay, livable, and complete. A series of cabinets, blue, yellow, and lilac lead to the only bedroom. . . . A table rises from a trap door in the dining room. Instead of swans, there are now fleurs-de-lys."

There was also a hut inspired by *Die Walküre*, where Ludwig and his suite, dressed in bearskins, drank mead from drinking horns, and, nearby, a Moorish kiosk which he bought at the 1867 Paris Exposition.

His other palaces became more and more extravagant (in one there are more than a hundred portraits of the *Roi Soleil*). Whole factories were commandeered to produce crockery and knickknacks that caught Ludwig's fancy. Hundreds of weavers worked frenziedly filling his orders for tapestries. Industriously, and with mad haste, he built his toy castles in mammoth proportions and fitted them out, like a good theater director, with appropriate props.

Such excessive zeal in making a theater of life, in living only for beauty and aesthetic sensation, is what attracts both artists and peasants to Ludwig, the fairy-tale king who spent his days consumed with the idea of his own majesty.

In his youth, Lindner made pilgrimages to Ludwig's castles. It is interesting, though, that the wild alps, the wooded foothills, the crystalline lakes beloved by so many Bavarians meant little to Lindner. There are no landscapes in his oeuvre, few allusions to great spaces or heights—there are only people, animals, and objects. Even as a boy, his interests were urban, his tastes for the enclosed spaces of the theater, the make-believe carried to its extreme.

Like Jean Cocteau, he has always liked "those beings who, incapable of creating masterpieces, try to become one in their own persons."[13]

Cocteau saw Ludwig II and his cousin the Empress Elizabeth as victims of that sickness. "To have mixed with men of genius, to praise and protect them was not enough for them. A black sun charred their souls."

Lindner's sympathy for such figures extends not only to King Ludwig, but to the numerous small-time actors and self-ordained prima donnas who throng his paintings. His respect for tragic eccentricity led him to try, for instance, to paint a portrait of Verlaine, but it never worked out. As Lindner says, his sympathy always turned into sentimentality. In the case of another grand eccentric, Marcel Proust, Lindner succeeded because it was clear "that one couldn't have sympathy with *him*."

The handling of the living friends in *The Meeting* is in keeping with the legendary character of the rest of the painting. They, too, share the mood of reverie, and they

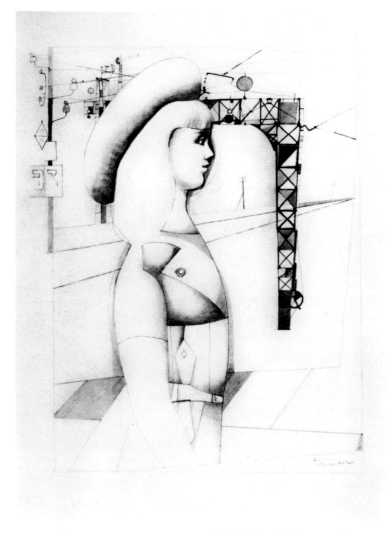

Plate 18. UNTITLED C. 1952. Pencil sketch for magazine illustration, 16 × 12″. Collection the artist

are distanced, made part of a past by means of their static poses, as though fixed by a camera.

Their presence in this painting commemorates the common past Lindner shares with them. Hedda Sterne and Saul Steinberg, at that time husband and wife, bring from their native Romania a vivid interest in the eccentric, the bizarre, the legendary. Miss Sterne is a romantic painter, concerned with poetic metaphor, and Steinberg, in his drawings, has always maintained his interest in the mores of the folk of any country. The understanding they brought to Lindner's early efforts was indispensable to him.

The third figure, Evelyn Hofer, is also of singular importance in his life. A refugee from Germany, Miss Hofer shared the numerous psychological problems of exile. Her work as an artist—she is an extraordinarily fine photographer—has been of considerable interest to Lindner, who has at times worked from her photographs.

All three shared with Lindner a determination to participate in American life; to understand and accept wholly the new circumstances in which history thrust them. They recognized and encouraged Lindner's talents, and helped him to make the essential break with his past as an illustrator. Lindner had been able to make a luxurious living almost from the day of his arrival in the United States by illustrating for such major magazines as *Vogue*, *Fortune*, and *Harper's Bazaar*, and also doing book jackets and illustrations (plate 18). His need to renounce art-by-assignment became increasingly urgent toward 1950. His friends encouraged his decision to cease all commercial activity and to concentrate on his own painting. When he took a modest job at Pratt Institute as an instructor, in 1952, they rejoiced, for they knew it was the beginning of Lindner's first true self-fulfillment.

Steinberg and Sterne have still another bond with Lindner: their Jewish consciousness. They were not only physically exiled, but exiled as Jews, in whom the Jewish heritage remained strong.

Lindner, being a German Jew, reared in an atmosphere of assimilation, seems not to have felt his Jewishness strongly before the advent of the Nazis. But the fact of being a Jew is important to him now. He mentions it often, and appears to credit much of his insight to his experience as a Jew.

The roots of this Jewishness can be traced to Bavaria. As the son of a comfortably established businessman, Lindner did not encounter anti-Semitism in its grosser manifestations. But he could not have grown up in

29

Nuremberg without being aware of Jews as separate and not wholly welcome residents.

As early as 1120, the chroniclers refer with hatred to the Nuremberg Jews who chose all the best sites for their houses. Around 1298, the Jewish quarter was in the center of town. The Jews there, and in neighboring towns, were massacred—as they were regularly in early Nuremberg history—some 100,000 of them. Again in 1349, their houses were destroyed and the Jews were burnt on St. Nicholas Eve.

In the fifteenth century, the French historian Froissart notes that "the hatred of the Jews is so general in Germany that the calmest of people are beside themselves when the conversation turns to their usury."[14]

On the tenth of March, 1499, the Jews once again were driven from their homes, which were sold by Maximilian to the town council, and they were not readmitted to Nuremberg until 1850.

The anti-Semitism in Bavaria waxed and waned, but never wholly disappeared. No matter how comfortable Lindner's life as an assimilated son of a German bourgeois family was, he must have felt the undertones. He might have heard little ditties such as "Though they smear caviar on our shoes / We won't be ruled by dirty Jews" during his childhood. And later, after World War I, he could hear the song: "By night I lie in my dear bed / By day I strike the Hebrew dead."

Immediately after the war, he could have seen posted on walls anxious declarations by the Jewish communities, pointing out how many sons they had lost in the Great War, and begging for consideration.

He was in Munich in 1923 when a film version of *Nathan the Wise* brought on anti-Semitic riots. (Nine years later, *All Quiet on the Western Front* sparked Nazi demonstrations, and a tragi-comic scene in the theater where the Nazis released hundreds of mice.)

The exiles, then, in *The Meeting* share with Lindner a special past and take their place as family, joined as families are, not so much by common interests (although in this case they are there) as by a common past.

LULU

The only character in *The Meeting* who survives nearly intact in Lindner's future work is the corseted maiden, significantly painted from behind, as though she were existent in a present gazing on a past.

Like everyone else in the picture, this character has a rich, often ambiguous, and greatly embellished past. Since she is certainly central—as Lindner paints her literally—to Lindner's entire oeuvre, she must be discussed in detail.

Although she appears, here, as a "principle" rather than as a flesh-and-blood woman, she was not always so. In the earlier representations, as in *Man and Woman* (plate 3), she is identifiable as the servant girl, plump, sexually magisterial like a ship's figurehead, and rather stupidly benign in expression. In the 1951 *Woman in Corset* (plate 19) she is cretinous, turgid, her hands dangle like a rag doll's, and the garters hang slack like the hands. She is far from being the determined, well-girt sexual aggressor she later becomes. She is the traditional housemaid who sleeps with father and son, and is a mere instrument of pleasure, or initiation.

But in *The Meeting* she is something more. She is an evocation of a long line of amoral sirens. There she stands, immobile, powerful, in the middle of life, a reincarnation of Wedekind's famous Lulu.

Lulu in the *Erdgeist (Earth Spirit)* and *Pandora's Box* is drawn as an innocent corruptress. The play is prefaced with a quote from Schiller: "I was created out of coarser stuff by nature, and desire draws me earthwards."

Men commit suicide, shoot each other, squabble over her, but she is the agent of forces that are chthonic, mysterious. Wedekind's Lulu—like the Lulus Lindner depicts, regardless of their changing costumes—is also a victim of the cowardice and hypocrisy of men. In the *Erdgeist*, Lulu explains to her lover's son that she has danced and was a model and was glad to earn her keep that way, but "to love to order is beyond me!" He in turn explains to her painter husband: "It's your fault and yours alone if you've failed hitherto to bring out the best in her."

Lulu then is a double figure—a sociological fact and an eternal principle. She tells her beggar father that she hasn't been called Lulu for a long time, and he answers: "As if the principle wasn't always the same."

All of Wedekind's male characters, like the males in Lindner's paintings, are weak, hypocritical, and equivocal. Their ruses and manipulations are in sharp contrast to Lulu's absolute candor. Wedekind believed that bourgeois society forces people to inhibit and pervert their natural instincts, of which Lulu is the personification. In a later play, he expressly states that "cultural institutions exist to be outgrown. . . . The free love market in which the tigress is triumphant is founded on an eternal law of immutable creation."[15]

Wedekind was a contemporary and friend of Strindberg's, and shared the preoccupations with the Feminine Principle of the late nineteenth-century Expressionists and Symbolists, among them Munch. His tart, rude style survived, and his view of women remained a widespread view in the Germany of Lindner's youth.

Lulu was everywhere. She was a legend in Bavaria, too, only her name was Lola Montez. Lola Montez, the corruptress of kings (she had seduced Ludwig's uncle), was a fabled figure in Bavaria, as commonly discussed as Ludwig.

Lulus by other names were salient in German theater,

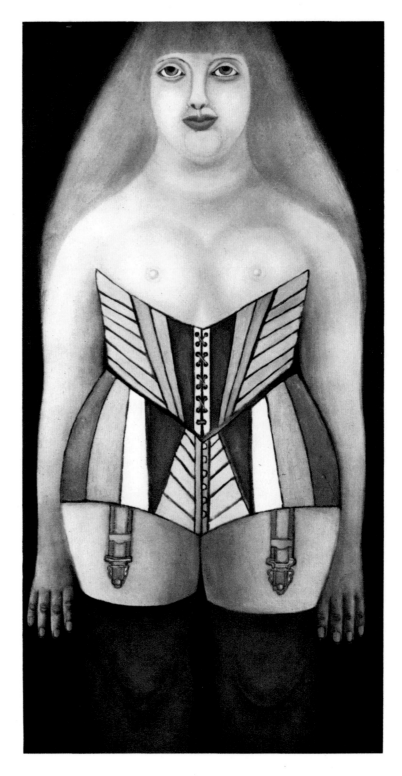

Plate 19. WOMAN IN CORSET. 1951. Oil on canvas, 40 × 20″.
Collection Mme André Bloc, Boulogne (Seine), France

opera, and films. Lola Lola in *The Blue Angel* is an example. Writers and painters and film makers were repeatedly drawn to the variety artiste, the prostitute or circus girl, outcasts of bourgeois society but admirable in their independence. (Beckmann painted them frequently, as did Léger and Picasso.)

The films of immediate postwar Germany were filled with crude versions of Lulu, and of their exploiters and victims. Titles such as *From the Verge of Swamps*, *Women Engulfed by the Abyss*, *Lost Daughters*, and *Hyenas of Lust* give the tenor of the times. Lindner while an art student often earned a little money by playing piano in the movie houses, and would have seen these potboilers.

Some of these films exploited the images of prewar writers such as Wedekind, although S. Kracauer notes a difference in the psychology: "The sex films testified to the primitive needs arising in all belligerent countries after war," he explains. "These films had nothing in common with the prewar revolt against outmoded sexual customs."[16]

As Lindner was so widely exposed to the arts of the first two decades of the twentieth century in Germany, it is probable that his attitude toward women and sex was conditioned. It was, and is still, part of the general cultural attitude that can be traced back to both the artistic and political events of his youth.

Lindner carries this attitude intact. For instance, he echoes the empathy Wedekind felt for his Lulu when he speaks of Marilyn Monroe. He sees her as a victim of Hollywood, a symbol of Hollywood's obsession with death and sex. "They made a little-girl image of her, and then they kept her in an icebox," he has remarked. "It was absolutely deathlike—Bellevue's morgue. They should have finished her off like they finished off Harlow."

The Lulu in *The Meeting* is bluntly stated. She is a material fact. There is no sentimentality in her stance,

her fully modeled limbs (indicating Lindner's interest in Léger), or in her mask: the cat's figure formed by the elaborate lacing of her corset. This, by the way, recurs often in Lindner's women, identifying them with the independence and natural cleverness of the feline.

Similarly, there was surprisingly little sentimentalism in Wedekind's view, where Lulu is presented as a being as natural as a cat or a tigress. This presentation of the female, which survives in Lindner's paintings today, is the product of a cultural attitude shaped by a large number of artists. Lindner merely extends a well-established tradition of assault on bourgeois morality via an exaggeration of unwelcome truths.

The gentility of German burgher attitudes survives in middle-class attitudes in the United States, at least on the surface. An artist who presents the vulgar in its highest, most shocking light is both feared and secretly admired, for the bourgeois is the first to delight in the forbidden pleasures of vulgarity.

Lindner belongs to a long line of artists, and particularly German artists, who have thrown their creative forces against the false walls of bourgeois morality.

Wedekind certainly used vulgar diction and types as weapons. He listened to the ballads and *Moritats*—those grisly recitals of murders, sex violations, and executions—in the hinterlands and found the harsh poetry of the people a source of power. Coarse slang, in his hands, became an expression of honesty—the shocking, salty spray of a truth rooted in the lives of those who almost never made an impression on the burgher classes, whose lives were carefully screened from view, and whose language was despised.

He was followed in this by Brecht, whose presence in Lindner's milieu might well have helped to shape Lindner's visions. Lindner was in Berlin in 1928–29, the time of *The Threepenny Opera*, a greatly discussed and widely influential event. Polly is another Lulu, observed by Brecht as Lulu had been observed by Wedekind, in the beer gardens and fair grounds of Bavaria.

Neither of the playwrights was concerned with personal involvement in describing what he saw. Martin Esslin writes of Brecht: "Like the ballads of the street singer, whose strident tones he tried to reproduce, most of the poems are reports on the accidents and crimes of other people, or dramatic monologues whose first person singular or plural is clearly that of historical or imagined characters." Even in his more autobiographical poems, such as *Poor B. B.*, Esslin points out, "the lyrical self-portrait of the author is put forward in the exhibitionist tone of a music hall performer presenting a character sketch, masking the private emotion by the posturing of a public performance."[17]

Lindner's sorties into the city, where the vulgar is rampant—his long tours in Macy's, his walks in Spanish Harlem, his rooting in the Lower East Side or in the great movie palaces—serve the same function. He makes note of the vernacular—the visual vernacular. He observes the postures, the choices of the housemaids on their Thursdays out. He makes note of their shoes, their gloves, their gestures. He watches the changing signs and emblems of the city, and includes their elementary language in his paintings. But his "news" is recast. What he tells of these women is of their never-changing appetites and their never-changing earthiness. Only their costumes change. Like the authors of plays and films, he abstracts and objectifies his visions.

His observations are dispassionate. The painted sirens are not erotic manifestations, but coolly observed erotic instruments, what the French so aptly call *machines à l'amour*. "We *feel* erotic attraction," Lindner once explained, speaking of the unlikely partners people so often choose. "Either we *look* or we *feel*. We don't do both. Looking is detached."

Plate 20. BOY. 1954. Pencil, 25 × 18″. Collection Mr. and Mrs. Richard L. Selle, Chicago, Illinois

BOY'S DREAMS

Although *The Meeting* was a decisive painting for Lindner, its cathartic value worked slowly. It was to be some time before his work was as New Yorkerish, as fully absorbed with the present, as his conscious mind already was in 1953. Many recapitulations, many experiments with style and imagery intervened.

There was his brief but intense preoccupation with children. Lindner's children are monsters of precocity. The suggestion is that they are perhaps the only grownups in the world. They know, but they know not what they know. The wise, sad, often demonic and bloated children in his paintings are small adults, and often they have distinct resemblance to the authority figures: dictators, kings, and matrons.

Most widely remarked when they were first exhibited were those softly fleshed boys and girls who resemble the overfed children in late nineteenth-century German postcards and valentines, porcelain dolls, or pathological types.[18]

As early as 1942, Lindner was playing with the image of the *Wunderkind*, seen as a sinister, half-mad miniature adult.[19] The physical characteristics in his more shocking portrayals (*Boy*, plate 20) follow quite closely the physical type established by the German psychiatrist Kretschmer, and published in a celebrated book, *Physique and Character*, in 1921.

Kretschmer, and many other investigators, used pathological subjects to investigate character types. The 1920s were a period of many attempts to generalize, and to find the "norm" in every situation. Kretschmer offered three basic types, the asthenic, the athletic, and the type portrayed by Lindner, the pyknic: "Pronounced peripheral development of the body cavities (head, breast and stomach) and a tendency to a distribution of fat about the trunk with a more graceful construction of the motor apparatus (shoulders and extremities)."

Probably Lindner's repulsive vision of the dreaming boy was inspired by another famous book, in which the art of the insane was discussed for the first time. This book, by Hans Prinzhorn, was one of Lindner's early pos-

sessions, and he still refers to it with reverence. He believes that the sources of art can be sensed in the work of psychotics and children—whom he always links. The turgid children in his paintings of the 1950s are in an obscure way the issue of this conviction, since they are, in their unhealthy tumescence, clearly abnormal, particularly the male children.

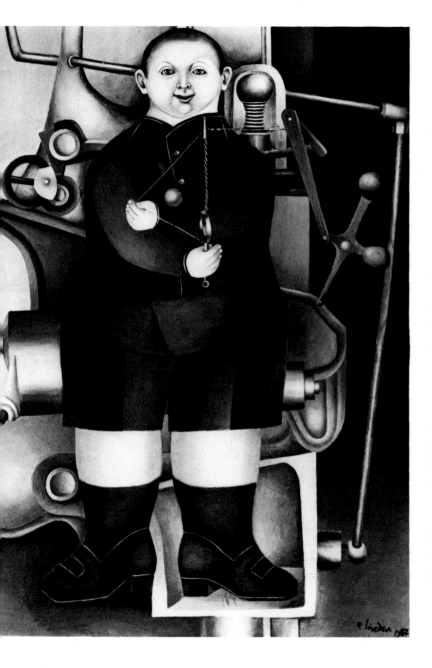

The little girls, like the sister in *The Meeting*, are languorous, plump, and provocative (*Girl Sitting*, plate 21). They have been compared with the adolescents of Balthus. They are immobile, knowing little women. Lindner clearly admires their *sang-froid*. Like women, who as Lindner says have secrets they don't even know they have, these adolescent girls have women's dreams.

Men, on the other hand, according to Lindner, have boys' dreams all their lives.

The boys' dreams took up several years in Lindner's oeuvre. In a sense, all his paintings are about boys' dreams.

The dreaming boy is often seen in these earlier works with his eyes closed or lowered. He is described first as

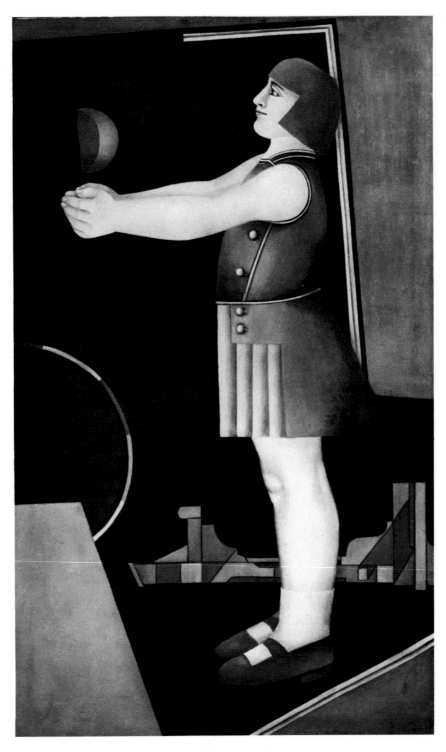

Plate 24. GIRL. 1955. Oil on canvas, 50 × 30″.
Cordier & Ekstrom, Inc., New York

a manipulator of toys and later as a wishful manipulator of women. The corset strings in so many subsequent paintings have an earlier history: they are the strings that pull the marionette-like or mechanical toys of the dreaming boys.

The *Boy with Machine* (plate 22) of 1954, for instance, pulls a string—an angular string—to activate his toy, or his reverie. One year later, Lindner paints the boy again (plate 23), this time on a circus stool, confined in the space of a marionette theater, stupidly at work to produce his vision.

His *Girl* (plate 24) of 1955, on the contrary, is now emancipated from her passive role. She stands firm. She is not doll-like. Her hands are large as they juggle with a half-moon ball. The carnival atmosphere is suggested by a low-lying abstraction in the rear, which might be circus tents, and by the giant child's hoop. While the boy is still enmeshed in his fantastic toys, the girl is out in the world.

Still, the relationship of boy and girl is not unambiguous. Until around 1960, Lindner occasionally takes a benign tone of reminiscence, and presents his children with only a faint trace of suggestiveness. *One Afternoon* (plate 25), of 1958, presents the girl and boy at their indoor games. He wears his sailor suit still, and his games are suggested by his clownlike make-up, the keyboard or game board that is superimposed on the girl's torso, and the baton he carries. The only suggestion of perversity is in the perhaps unconscious styling of the girl's boots, with their spurlike appendages, and in the screen above, which suggests a boudoir.

It is in 1958, the year of this painting, that Lindner's painting style undergoes a sharp conversion. He no longer describes close chambers with low ceilings, but allows the space to open out. He begins to play with integrated abstract shapes, pushing them in and around his characters to suggest the complexity of their actions.

Plate 25.
ONE AFTERNOON. 1958.
Oil on canvas, 40 × 30″.
Cordier & Ekstrom, Inc., New York

The human figure is now seen as dissectable, as diagrammatic, as an authentic machine.

Lindner tried out a number of approaches. He left behind the subdued tonal treatment, so much like a photograph, as he left behind his reminiscences. *One Afternoon* is painted thickly and dominated by rich, abstract areas of scarlet and purple. As in another 1958 painting, *The Window* (plate 66), there are forms that are there for their own sake, interlocking and engaging the eye in yet another "content."

Critics have called this an essay into Cubism. Unquestionably, the flattened spaces indicate the assimilation of Cubist devices. But far more than any orthodox Cubist, Léger impressed Lindner, and it is more likely that it was through Léger's manner that Lindner emancipated himself from his earlier literalism.

Léger's attitude toward the things around him such as hammers and nails, which he took, according to Lindner, and made into symbols, shaped Lindner's own attitude. He says that Léger, especially during his most Cubist phase, was his greatest teacher largely because "Léger had no European sentimentalities. He was innocent of art history. He said, 'I like these objects *as such*,' and painted them." Lindner in the early 1950s occasionally renders his homage to Léger openly, as when he paints one of Léger's favorite motifs, the bicycle rider.

As for the human figure, Léger early saw its parallels with other mechanisms. In his experimental film *Ballet Mécanique*, 1924, he played with equalizing objects and living organisms. His own commentary on his film activities, published in 1926, amounts to an aesthetic credo—one that Lindner understood:

"A pipe—a chair—an eye—a typewriter—a hat—a foot, etc. etc. Let us consider these things for what they can contribute to the screen just as they are—in isolation—their value enhanced by every known means.

"In the enumeration I have purposely included parts of the human body in order to emphasize the fact that in the new realism the human being, the personality, is very interesting only in these fragments and that these fragments should not be considered of any more importance than any of the other objects listed."

Léger's attitude toward the treatment of the human figure in films was carried over into his own painting in varying degrees. Despite his interest in objects, Léger never quite subordinated the human figure. Nor does Lindner. Yet, in 1958, when he first renounced the theater enclosure, he dispersed the solids in his painting with experimental abandon.

Films, incidentally, are as important to Lindner as they were to Léger. He is a faithful movie-goer in New York, and an assiduous student of television. Knowing that he was among the enthusiasts for the new German films after the war, several critics have responded to his work by associating him with Expressionist films, above all *The Cabinet of Dr. Caligari*. There are certainly some justifiable comparisons to be made. For instance, the relevance of circular motifs, both abstract and real, as in the merry-go-round. In the later *Dr. Mabuse*, as Kracauer points out, there are insistently circular ornaments, which Kracauer maintains are symbols of chaos.[20]

His comments on Walter Ruttman's editing of *Berlin, die Symphonie einer Grosstadt*, released in 1927, which was an event of importance in Weimar Germany, stress both the interest in mechanization and the impressions of chaos Ruttmann achieved. He says the editor relies on the formal qualities of objects rather than on their meanings. Machine parts which appear throughout the film are cut in such a manner that they turn into dynamic displays of an almost abstract character. Furthermore, "symbols of chaos that first emerged in postwar films are here resumed and supplemented by other pertinent symbols. Conspicuous in this respect is a unit of successive shots combining a roller coaster, a rotating spiral in a shop window, and a revolving door."

These circular motifs are constant in Lindner's work. First in the hoops, sparklers, and gear-driven toys. Later in the targets ubiquitous from the mid-1950s on. Already in the 1958 *Stranger No. 1* (plate 63) the carnival begins to be transformed into the city. Dotted lines and other emblems of city life intersect the female figure—a rudimentary suggestion of the pulsating dynamism of the city.

Lindner's concentration at this time on the figure as a mechanism, or as a mechanical diagram, as in *Stranger No. 2* (plate 65) with its "cut out here" dotted lines, its arrows, and its implication of three-dimensionality, probably has its source far back in his memory. He has said that while he was a student in Munich, he was not moved by the legacy of the only important avant-garde movement of the generation before, the Blue Rider, but rather by the publication of the work of Duchamp and Picabia.

Both of these artists had excelled in the use of engraved mechanical diagrams as analogues for the human figure, and both represented the new spirit of rejection congenial to a youth in the chaos of Weimar Germany. The absurd, the challenging, fitted the times far more than the yearning idealism and violent emotion of the Expressionists.

Although Lindner was in Munich when the postwar Dadaist revival occurred in Berlin, its reverberations reached him. The great questions posed by the Dadaists activated his imagination. For the first time, he recounts, he and everyone else had to question the continuity of art—question, in fact, its very existence.

He has never ceased questioning. Echoes of Dada skepticism occur in his few public statements, such as the following, published in a Museum of Modern Art catalogue:

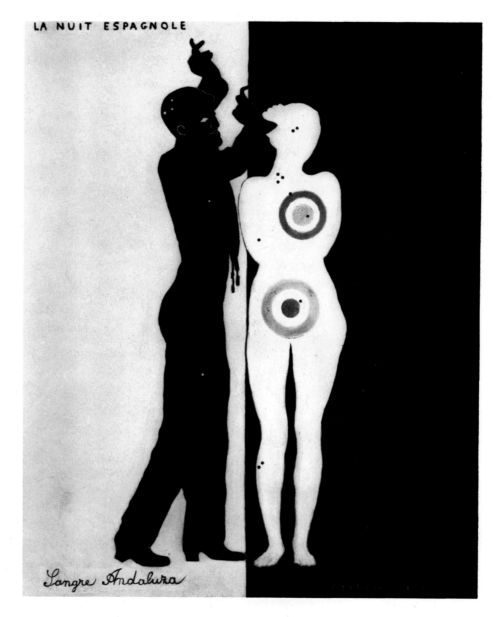

Plate 26. Francis Picabia. LA NUIT ESPAGNOLE. 1922. Oil on canvas, 72 × 59″. Private collection, New York

"I cannot talk about painting.

"I have now even doubts that there is such a thing as art in general.

"More and more I believe in the secret behavior of human beings. Maybe all of us are creative if we listen to the secret of our inner voice."[21]

The attraction of Dada publications, with their eruptive typography and their queer juxtapositions of machinery with the human physiology, was one of the few influences that Lindner can cite decisively as important in his formation as an artist. He often reiterates his debt to Duchamp, and especially to Picabia. Coming from rather a different environment, and with sharply differing spiritual roots, Lindner shares a surprising number of preoccupations of World War I vintage with Picabia. He may have seen some of Picabia's early collages and drawings, such as *De Zayas!*, described by William Camfield as "a symbolic machine portrait of Marius de Zayas . . . chiefly derived from schematic diagrams of electrical systems: however, Picabia has devised his own system incorporating heterogeneous items which . . . can be partly identified as: an empty corset joined by a line from the region of the heart to what appears to be a gigantic spark plug in a ventilating apparatus, a hand crank, and two automobile headlights . . . with a female plug between them that eventually connects to the empty corset (as does the hand crank) at its point of sex."[22]

Picabia was also greatly enamored of the target, usually associated with the female body in a symbolical way. His 1922 *La Nuit Espagnole* (plate 26), which was widely remarked when it was first exhibited, might have been familiar to Lindner during the 1920s. At any rate, he distinctly remembers being impressed by it in the 1930s. The comparison of certain paintings, such as *The Target* of 1959 (plate 72) and *La Nuit Espagnole*, reveals direct affinities.

If the Dadaist spirit interested Lindner in his twenties, so did other more positive expressions of new concepts, particularly in theater. He saw the experimental performances in Piscator's Proletarian Theater, founded in 1919 in Berlin. He recalls the excitement of going to the theater "as if you were going to secret revolutionary meetings." He was impressed and a little frightened by the atmosphere. Recalling Brecht he says: "He was already very avant-garde looking, like a thief or a secret agent. He was a revolutionary without a revolution. (The Germans are very inventive.) He wore his hair short and a leather jacket, and behaved as if he were in a secret cell meeting."

In this theater, Lindner would have seen the first daring use of films within a representation. He would have seen many plays based on the conflict of men and machines (particularly Toller's *Masses and Men*, and Kaiser's plays). He would have seen sets in which wires and strings indicated the various planes of action, or, as in Toller's *Hoppla, Such Is Life* (1927), a drama enacted on a scaffolding divided into several floors, with "Cinematographic prelude: noises, alarm bells, flashes of light. . . ." Or Kaiser's *Gas II*, with its stage directions: "Concrete Hall. Light falls in dusty beams from arc lamp. From misty height of dome dense wires horizontally to iron platform, thence diagonally distributed to small iron tables, three right, three left. Red wires to the left, green to the right. At each table a Figure in Blue—seated stiffly, uniformed, gazing into glass pane in the table which, lighting up, reflects its color on the face above it, red to the left, green to the right. Across and farther down, a longer iron table chequered like a chessboard with green and red plugs operated by the first figure in blue. . . ."

There are several aspects of Piscator's program of interest in relation to Lindner. For one, as he wrote in 1929, Piscator—radically—banned the word "art."[23] His suspicion of the bourgeois associations with "art" was shared by most artists in the middle 1920s who emphatically rejected the kind of hypocritical reverence paid "art" by philistine bourgeois.

Furthermore, Piscator, carrying out a long line of imperatives issued from Hölderlin to Wedekind, tried to deal with the vernacular, the vulgar, in a meaningful way. This led to his emphasis on journalism: "My idea in those days was a much closer connection with journalism, with day-to-day affairs." He placed great stress on observation and on the principle of reporting. The emphasis was on documentation and contemporaneity in his productions.

Lindner's own practice of day-to-day journalism, becoming more salient all the time, is a contemporary extension of this old principle first explored with genius by Piscator in the 1920s.

Still another development in German theater must be mentioned. The theater of the Bauhaus, and particularly the work of Oskar Schlemmer, moved in a cooler, more abstract direction but was nevertheless of considerable importance in Weimar Germany. Lindner, living in Bavaria, had no opportunity to see the Bauhaus performances. But he would certainly have heard all about them, and possibly have seen reproductions of Schlemmer's designs. In any case, the ideas put forward by the various members of the Bauhaus were deposited deeply in German culture, and would have had an effect on any sensitive theater-goer, no matter how indirectly.

In Bauhaus conceptions, the mechanization of the human figure was a prime preoccupation. A whole rhetoric was developed to expound the concept of the *Kunstfigur*, which Schlemmer traces from Hoffmann's machine to Kleist's important essay on marionettes. The *Kunstfigur*, Schlemmer explained in "Mensch und Kunstfigur," permits any kind of movement and any kind of position. In his theater, "everything which can be mechanized *is* mechanized. The result: our recognition of that which *cannot* be mechanized." In treating the figure both as an abstract entity and in its natural state, Schlemmer felt that "endless perspectives are opened up: from the supernatural to the nonsensical, from the sublime to the comic."[24]

Schlemmer's early and extraordinary *The Triadic Ballet*, first conceived in 1912 but performed completely only in 1922 in Stuttgart, is filled with Chirico-like recessions, padded costumes making his characters into robot dolls, and a multitude of symbolic props.

Even the scenario description of his 1922 *Figural Cabinet I* graphically establishes his style, and the elements within it that were influential:

"Half shooting gallery—half *metaphysicum abstractum*. Medley, i.e., variety of sense and nonsense, methodized by Color, Form, Nature, and Art; Man and Machine; Acoustics and Mechanics. . . . In the midst the Master, E.T.A. Hoffmann's Spalanzani, spooking around, directing, gesticulating, telephoning, shooting himself in the head. . . . Imperturbably the window-shade roller unwinds, showing colored squares, and arrows and other signs, commas, parts of the body, numbers, advertisements. . . ."

Photographs of the first performance of the *Figural Cabinet* show the use of a *lingua franca* of signs and devices then shared by artists all over Europe. The figures are like mannequins. Typographic signs appear to express their mechanized status. There are floating question marks, and lines connecting machine forms that are very similar to those in Picabia's drawings. There are targets, whirlers, and pie-shaped color charts. And there are the metallic figures Schlemmer describes as whizzing and dashing on wires from background to foreground.

The common vocabulary is reflected also in Moholy-Nagy's concept of total theater. He describes a hectic stage on which "arrows plunge, louvered shutters open up, disks rotate, electric apparatus, lightning, thunder, grid systems of colors shoot up, down, back, forth, wheels, explosions, odors, clownery, mechanical men. . . ."[25]

Even though the Dada spirit was essentially alien to the social aims of Piscator's group and the theater of the

Bauhaus, the tremendous freedom of innovation evident during the 1920s was partly brought about by Dada's persistent challenge to old values. Certainly it was the spirit of Dada which inspired George Grosz, for instance, when he designed the sets for Ivan Goll's *Methusalem* in 1922 (plate 27). Yet, his pictorial vocabulary differs little from the sets described by Schlemmer or Moholy-Nagy.

In these various descriptions of theater devices of the early 1920s, Lindner's vocabulary is recognizable. The elements of the language of the 1920s survive in his work of the late 1950s. His manipulation of the human figure,

treated—as in *Stranger No. 2* (plate 65)—as a doll with movable parts, is far more closely related to similar experiments in theater than it is to Cubist analysis.

In *The Target*, 1959, the disks are clearly intended as targets, similar to the shooting-gallery target in Picabia's *La Nuit Espagnole*. The male figure is reduced to a diagrammatic shadow on a backdrop. By contrast, the woman is exaggerated, a lofty mannequin whose corset string is being pulled somewhere outside the picture. The string, oddly enough, is broken at an angle, much as are the strings in the several versions of boys with machines, suggesting the boy's erotic mechanical fancies even in his absence.

The new woman all but dominates the foreground. Her stockinged legs are emphasized, while her armor is painted with more precision and invention than previously. Still, she is not quite yet the New York girl of the streets. Her features are neutral and in her leggy height and broad hips she is still related to the classical Bavarian servant-girl type.

Lindner's play with abstract shape here (the half-moon, the round knees, the breasts, and the targets) and in other paintings of that period—for instance *The Keyboard* (plate 80), in which the woman becomes a keyhole, while the bust of a pompous nineteenth-century gentleman is sliced up into the curves of a piano which are then repeated behind the keyhole woman—slowly clarified his intentions. His narrative impulse is checked by an instinctive feeling for painterly play, and the two begin to find their balance by about 1960.

Still, the reverie mood is not entirely dissipated. From time to time, Lindner paints an ensemble picture, a synoptic résumé of his various concerns up to that point, and one of these is *The Secret* (plate 28), a distinctly theatrical image.

Here we have the dreaming schoolboy again, at lower right, his eyes closed and his hand holding the imaginary

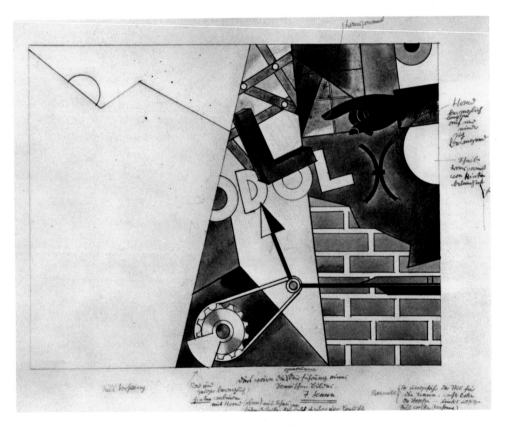

Plate 27. George Grosz. STAGE DESIGN FOR IVAN GOLL'S METHUSALEM. 1922. Ink and watercolor, 15 1/2 × 20 1/4″. Peter H. Deitsch Gallery, New York

Plate 28.
THE SECRET. 1960. Oil on canvas,
50×40″. Collection Myron Orlofsky,
White Plains, New York

string which activates the girl. She trips unconcernedly within her circle. She is the old china-doll type of his earlier paintings, with small hands and helmetlike coiffure, a schoolgirl in a middy blouse. (She is, for all her schoolgirl neutrality, still Lulu. When an admirer asks Wedekind's Lulu "what difference it could make if instead of this rabble you had only *one* spectator," she answers promptly: "It would make no difference at all. I never notice anyone.")

The schoolboy is also present in a vignette—as though on a platform on the stage—as the onlooker, the stranger, the *Ceremoniemeister*. He is in an aperture watching himself dreaming, so to speak.

These large spaces within which Lindner's characters here perform foretell his later clarifications of the picture plane. His experiment with small and disparate parts is not over yet, but by 1960 he has decided to keep the human figures prominent and not equal with other elements in his paintings. He has also injected a note of sharpness which is felt increasingly after this. The dreaming schoolboy alternates in the late 1950s with the city slicker, the real voyeur, and the softening effects of reminiscences gradually give way to the acuity of day-to-day journalism.

If Lindner worked, as I believe he did, from a chronological sequence of moods and experiences in his past, then by the 1960s he had worked through his German past but was still reacting to the exile years in France.

The Paris Lindner found when he left Germany in 1933 was outwardly very much like the Paris he had enjoyed as a long-term visitor a few years before. The cafés were still the point of congregation. Artists and writers lived meanly but contentedly in ancient hotels, taking their meals in convenient neighborhood restaurants and piling up the saucers for their liqueurs and coffee in the cafés. It was like the Paris he had first known, "like the time of Modigliani. There was a Proust smell. The old behavior

was still there. I saw Gertrude Stein and Picasso. In Paris, you were where you belonged in those days. I lived in Montparnasse. Like everyone else, I had a *quartier*. Café, ink, paper, and that was enough for a whole day."

There was still considerable carry-over from the late 1920s, when France was feverishly trying to purge its memory of the dreadful Great War.

"People wanted to enjoy life peacefully. . . . Jazz bellowed late into the night and mobs admired the syncopated rhythm. Women wore very short skirts and said that they adored sport. Dancing, boxing matches, coachloads of tourists, vacuum cleaners, crosswords, and a number of other innovations made their appearance. Snobs who not so long ago had taken part in scrimmages at the First Nights of Diaghilev's ballets or at the Private Views of the Salon des Indépendants now frenziedly yelled 'Bravo, Joe!' at boxing matches."[26]

It was the era of the journalist writers, those who turned to the boxing matches and bicycle marathons for their subjects, and who wandered all over the world casting ironic eyes upon whatever they saw that was alien to European culture.

It was, when Lindner first arrived, still a country of spiritual refuge. The School of Paris, although waning, was still a reality. The Surrealists were having their second coming, the abstract artists were beginning to fight back against the realism that had already crept back into painting in the mid-twenties, and life went on as usual.

But only for a short time. Lindner, and the others who had hastily left Germany in 1933, soon found that the life of an exile is not the same as the life of a voluntary expatriate. Lindner found himself in a community of countrymen, none of whom could imagine that the Nazis would not be overthrown, and all of whom thought they would go back.

The Social Democrats, Lindner's party and one of the largest socialist parties in the world at that time, had been curiously sluggish in their reading of the signs of the times. From the very beginning of the Weimar Republic they had hoped for the best. Their more radical colleagues were murdered; political leaders of the Left disappeared; and the three German armies—one official and the other two tacitly permitted—were functioning smoothly.

Even when they fled after the burning of the Reichstag they hoped for the best. Every little shift had encouraged them before: in 1927 they had pointed out that Hitler's party had won only 40,000 votes, and in 1928, only 810,000 and 12 seats in the Reichstag. And in 1930, that he had only six million followers, and less than a majority in the Reichstag; and even in 1932, that he had lost rather than gained votes. They had hoped for the best.

For a whole year the *émigrés*, among them Lindner, acted as though their government-in-exile were functioning. It was not until the Rohm Putsch, in 1934, that these Social Democrats began to fear the worst.

Meanwhile, the rising tide of Fascism was touching France. The Croix de Feu and the Camelots du Roi, both extreme right-wing nationalist groups, staged demonstrations in Paris and behaved with the hoodlumlike license of their fellow Fascists in Italy and Germany. The French, like the Social Democrats in Germany, were not very vigorous in their fight against reaction.

Lindner and the others, cloistered by language and background, would have felt in this rising tide the antipathy for foreigners that from time to time surfaces in France with ugly results. As tension mounted, and more refugees poured in, changes were wrought.

"As a refugee in Paris, I changed my personality. We were the first exiles. But my generation was unfamiliar with exile—not like the Polish and Russian Jews. For us it was a real shock."

Life for Lindner, and for many other artists and writers in Paris at the time, was vague and unfocused. Unrest and political anxiety invaded the spirits of nearly everyone, and a surprising number of artists almost ceased to work. As Lindner puts it: "Time was very abstract for us. It was an uncontrollable situation of time. Look at Hitler: He was talking of a thousand years!" Time hung heavy, because nearly every thinking person knew, by 1936 or 1937, that war was imminent, and some already knew in 1933.

Reviewing his life before he came to America, Lindner often injects the problem of time and its illusory quality to him in relation to the events people call political. When he discusses his student years he is always vague, explaining that the series of shocks, beginning with World War I, were responsible for a general "fogginess" in him. Nothing seemed quite real because it was clear to him and his generation that it would not be quite permanent. Paradoxically, the "tempo was so slow in Bavaria that Hitler was there in no time."

Even while he was employed as art director for an important publishing firm in Munich, Lindner felt he was marking time and the "fogginess" prevailed in his life.[27] His own work was continually shunted to one side as he and others in Munich waited for the worst. Many intellectuals and painters frequenting the artists' cafés in Munich, where, Lindner says, Hitler came often and knew everyone by sight, knew even before 1930 that the Peace of Versailles would never hold.

The distortion of time, regretfully noted by Lindner, is no longer a problem. He thinks of the war of 1941 as a hundred years ago, while the wars he witnesses as an American are distant from an orderly, regulated life in which he feels secure. Or at least he feels that he belongs to New York. Since he first discovered that he belonged to this city, around 1960, he claims that for the first time he really understood his surroundings; he really experienced an unwarped sense of time, and his curiosity was permitted, finally, to function to its full capacity. This he could not have done in Paris, where his status as an alien was constantly brought home to him.

Still, Lindner in those first years looked for the "smell" of Paris. He did "research" on Proust, looking up people who knew him, talking to the man in the bookstore where Proust used to sit around, asking about Proust's movements, how he dressed, how he sat. "He was vain in his suits and his trousers were not crumpled," was what Lindner discovered.

As the atmosphere changed—the Popular Front government failed within a year and a half, and the Fascist movements took heart again—life became increasingly difficult for the refugees. The Spaniards were sequestered in concentration camps. The Germans were refused work permits. (Lindner survived only because his wife worked for *Vogue*.) The police began to harass the *émigrés*, and nasty incidents occurred in the streets.

The nightmare of documents began. Foreigners were required to have countless documents in order to remain in France, and very often the French bureaucracy would refuse them the necessary papers. When the hero in Kesten's novel, *The Twins of Nuremberg*, visited the prefecture, the official explained to him that the fact that he was an enemy of Hitler meant that he was conspiring against a government with which France was on diplomatic terms. When in 1938 Von Ribbentrop visited Paris, the French police rounded up the *émigrés*, who, they said, needed protective custody. And besides, all *émigrés* were potential terrorists.

"The moment one country became barbaric," Kesten observed bitterly, "every other country followed suit. One day condemning barbarians in the first country, they aped them the very next day in their own. The moment a dictator perpetrated a new piece of villainy, all the 'civilized' countries repeated it immediately. The genuine idealists of the vulgar twentieth century—both men and women, who sacrificed their lives, their fortunes, their health, their families, their fatherland, their careers, to an Idea—they became the toy of every informer in the democratic countries. Those who had the luck to escape their native tyrants were clapped into the prisons of the free countries, sometimes on the denunciations of the Consuls of their native tyrants. . . ."[28]

Before the French capitulated wholly to the demands of the Nazis, there were a few months of waiting. The Deux Magots continued to attract Picasso, Derain, Ehrenburg, Tzara, Heinrich Mann, Hemingway. "Half the guests knew each other," Kesten reports. "Among them were the most famous writers, professors from the nearby university, Berlin and Viennese literary lights, Spanish Republicans in exile, and a few anti-Fascists. There were also Giraudoux and Jules Romains, Count Sforza; the former Chancellor of the Reich, Joseph Wirth, Honneger and Maillol. . . ."

But the waiting was soon over. The French police dutifully filled their dossiers on enemies of the Third Reich, preparing to turn them over to the conquerors. Some political refugees were even expelled on demands from the German government. France as the refuge of the civilized had ceased to exist.

For Lindner, as for the others, life became an ugly repetition of life in Germany. Along with his countrymen and scores of French left-wingers, he was arrested and detained in the Sports Palace in 1939.

From the day of his arrest until his embarkation in Lisbon for New York in March, 1941, Lindner lived precariously, sharing the tragic and chaotic destiny of Europe in wartime, and doubly threatened in France as a German and as a Jew.

First he was interned in a French detention camp, where he defied his jailors by refusing to work. Soon he was given an opportunity to join the Foreign Legion.

He and a few other young German prisoners were put in trucks and driven nonstop to Marseilles, where, he discovered, every sergeant was a German, and where it seemed likely he would not survive. By outwitting the regimental doctor, he had himself shipped back to the same detention camp at Blois, where he again refused to do agricultural work. After a few weeks, war was officially declared.

Like many others, Lindner asked to volunteer. His adventures with a French regiment, where as a German he was regarded with suspicion, led to serious difficulties, and he soon escaped, joining a wandering Spanish company. Not long after, they were all caught by the French who were already under German command, and Lindner had the experience—which he rarely talks about—of being put against the wall to be shot.

His escape from death was a matter of moments. Thereafter, as the Germans closed in, his life was the life of a fugitive, moving by night and hiding by day, burying his papers when the military approached, unearthing them when the coast was clear. His flight to Free France—a nightmare all too common for millions of Jews—was on foot, terrifying, undermined by the mounting panic among the French, who would not stop to ask for papers but would shoot at anyone with a foreign accent.

Even when he reached the so-called Free Zone, Lindner existed in constant anxiety and had to shift his sleeping arrangements nightly to avoid the French agents of the Gestapo. His adventures continued. He watched hideous human events. He helped a converted Jewish abbé bring Jewish refugees to safety. He had a hideout in Marseilles where he familiarized himself with one of the most elaborate and tough underworlds in existence. He was in touch with the underground. He helped other German émigrés with their struggle to get papers. He witnessed countless murders.

And he himself experienced the numbness, the almost pathological indifference to death that overtakes those whose lives are at stake.

When he finally reached Lisbon, he saw even more sordid human abuse. The panic-stricken refugees besieged the various embassies, where they were met with cool, bureaucratic formality. Lives were haggled for, exchanged, and often lost in the delaying tactics employed by all too many governments.

At times, bodies of refugees who had been murdered for their boat tickets were found. In this atmosphere of mad fear and last hope, human frailties turned ugly, and Lindner, disheartened, stored up his bitter impressions.

NEW YORK

The experience with the fatal habits of bureaucrats given power over life and death was not lost. When Lindner had his first New York exhibition, in 1954, there were ample references to the hateful petty officials and to militaristic patriots. Titles in that show included *Marche Militaire*; *Académie Française* (plate 29); *The Academician* (plate 30)—all references to his French experience. One of the paintings, *The Juggler* (plate 47), shows a figure partly clad in clown's colors, partly in military uniform. He lowers his eyes in idiotic acquiescence. He is entranced, and the ball, suspended in the foreground, bears little relationship to him. He is a clown, and was probably not intended as a political comment, and yet, willing it or not, Lindner offers a cruelly disturbing vision that might very well have germinated during those last, agonizing years in Paris.

The Atlantis of his soul never interested Lindner consciously. Although reared in the era of Freudian analysis, he determinedly avoided analysis and self-

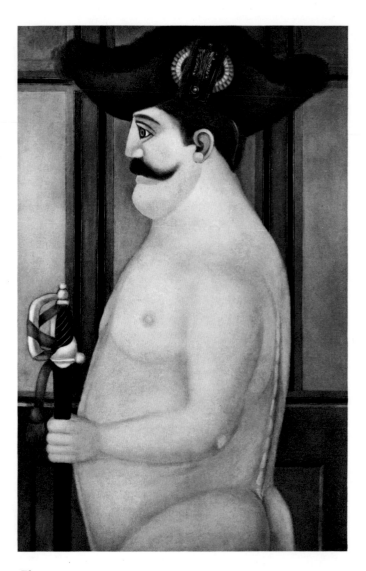

Plate 29. ACADÉMIE FRANÇAISE. 1950–61.
Oil on canvas, 39 × 29 1/2″. Collection
Mr. and Mrs. Henry A. Markus, Chicago, Illinois

Plate 30. THE ACADEMICIAN. 1951.
Oil on canvas, 40 × 26″. Collection
Miss Helen Mary Harding, New York

analysis. His assimilation of vocabulary, his sequestering of significant experiences, his "journalism" were
all effected without his conscious effort. How he put these
together, especially after 1960, is what constitutes his
unique power. Like the child whom he so vividly admires,
Lindner likes to save things, hide them away, so that
they may later surprise him. The surge of bitterness his
experience of the 1930s brought upon him was to emerge
twenty years later with surprising fervor.

His arrival in New York coincided with a strong, bur-

geoning movement in painting, but at first he was only
a witness. Although Lindner was acquainted with many
of the painters of the Abstract Expressionist movement,
and although he followed their work with interest, he
was not in any way intimate with them. He didn't visit
The Club, he didn't hang out at the Cedar Bar, he was
not on drinking terms with Jackson Pollock and Franz
Kline. Moreover, his work showed almost no response
to their doctrines.

Yet, he thinks of himself as an "action painter." He

explains that he shared with the Abstract Expressionists a desire to work without hesitation and strong conscious reflection. "I don't know myself, I don't want to know myself. I have a constant surprise when I work."

This emphasis on the surprise as the painting emerges is consciously related to his American painting colleagues in Lindner's mind. And it is, I suspect, motivated by the same need to reject the great French shadows that appeared in the early work of the Abstract Expressionists. Lindner's experience in France—a France that was decomposing visibly during those last years before the war—must have left a deep revulsion in him. Along with the German experience, the French experience had to be purged.

It was appropriately swallowed up by New York. When New York began to emerge as the fulcrum of Lindner's musings, Europe, and more particularly France, receded more and more.

New York as a theme puts in its appearance tentatively in the late 1950s. By 1961, it is more insistent. We find the carnival barker transformed, in an early version of *Coney Island* (plate 90), for instance, into an American gangster stereotype, with evil mustache, flashy suit, and a slightly out-of-date air. The same is true of the new Lulu. Lulu's progress is fast in these years. In *The Walk* (plate 91), she is a gauntleted whore of rather metallic distinction. She dominates the picture plane, and her environment is theatrical, with flats behind used to set her off. Her hat is a helmet, her corset is armor, her skirt is steely, and she has something of the 1940s in her manner. The point is, she is an *American* whore, a New York whore. And she is fancifully rendered with the cold precision once identified by the term "magic realism."

She reminds us that Lindner was in his early twenties when a brief but important chapter in European art, and particularly German art, was inscribed in twentieth-century art history. In 1923, Dr. G. F. Hartlaub, director of the Mannheim Kunsthalle, noticed the strongly increasing tendency in painting toward what he called positive, tangible reality. Painters all over Europe had drawn away from the frenzied experiments of just before and after the war. In Italy, the Valori Plastici group put forward their ideal of classical realism, which harked back to the clean, hard-surfaced renderings of the Early Renaissance. The Valori Plastici group itself was rather conservative and certainly mild in its pronouncements, but their influence—mainly in Germany—brought forward more violent expressions.

It was to the harsh paintings of that period by Otto Dix, George Grosz, and Max Beckmann that Hartlaub addressed himself, and for their exhibition in 1925 he coined the term *Neue Sachlichkeit*, translated in English as New Objectivity. In a much-quoted letter published in *Arts* in 1931, Dr. Hartlaub explained that the term "was related to the general contemporary feeling in Germany of resignation and cynicism after a period of exuberant hopes. . . . Cynicism and resignation are the negative side of the *Neue Sachlichkeit*; the positive side expresses itself in the enthusiasm for the immediate reality as a result of the desire to take things entirely objectively on a material basis without immediately investing them with ideal implications."

For German painters, with such immaculate precedents as Otto Runge in their backgrounds, the clean-lined, harshly lighted realism was an antidote to the ambiguities and romanticisms of the Expressionists. It is evident in Beckmann's self-portraits of the period and in his stern representations of girls of the streets and night-clubs; in Grosz's caricatures of the bourgeoisie; and in Dix's portraits, particularly of children.

Lindner was not attracted to the New Objectivity or its painters. Yet its basic motivations are not alien to him. (Apropos of Dix's children, he once pointed out that they were not as good as Runge's, whose children were angels, because they were the products of conscious Freudianism.) Lindner's objections to the New Objectivity painters are curious. He reproaches them with their attitude toward women: "They only painted prostitutes, like good German bourgeois husbands, prostitutes with painted faces." He, on the other hand, although he has never said so, paints Lulu from the Wedekind point of view—she is the innocent corruptress and not the dirty lure of the hypocritical bourgeois husband.

From another point of view, the increasingly highlighted, harshly characterized figures in Lindner's work of the early 1960s is perfectly in harmony with American painting tendencies. He moves out of the past into the present, ever sharpening and contemporizing his images. The china-doll temptresses are transformed into miniskirted Lolitas. Instead of servant girls, with their coarse limbs, there are secretaries impersonating call girls. He is using the material he sees day by day.

The new element in American art, after the first overwhelming tide of Abstract Expressionism, was an art that looked for the reality, the tangible reality of which Hartlaub spoke. This art, variously represented, came to be called Pop art.

Shortly after, another element was remarked, an abstract version of the same hard objectivity, in which exactitude replaced ambiguity and unmixed high color replaced tonal impastos.

Both of these tendencies can be linked with the earlier New Objectivity quite conveniently. Like their German predecessors, the young artists were surfeited with the idealistic programmes of the Abstract Expressionists. They doubted the validity of philosophy in relation to the material facts of painting. They were wary of the hysterical edge in the Abstract Expressionist voice which basically advocated salvation through love, just as their Expressionist brothers had forty years before. The hard-headed new artists preferred the unvarnished truth, and less lofty goals. They liked the vernacular, and they liked laicity. They did not believe in high priests and high art.

Even the historical circumstances had certain common features. The German New Objectivity advocates had lived through the Inflation and had seen the wild chaos of a disintegrated society. They were working in a newly affluent society—a society that had hit bottom and was hell-bent on preserving its new security.

The New Objective artists in the United States were also working in a relatively new affluence. The hungry bohemia which was the natural habitat of the Abstract Expressionist was unknown to them. They were participating in a highly materialist epoch and, while duly suspicious, they met it with a matching point of view.

In the Germany of the middle to late 1920s, the deceptive affluence was accompanied by a strong realistic current in the arts. S. Kracauer in his commentary on New Objectivity in films considered the attitude one marking a state of paralysis. "Cynicism, resignation, disillusionment: these tendencies point to a mentality disinclined to commit itself in any direction. The main feature of the new realism is its reluctance to ask questions, to take sides. Reality is portrayed not so as to make facts yield their implications, but to drown all implications in an ocean of facts."[29]

I think this criticism can be leveled justly at many American artists whose noncommittal stance is similar, and whose reliance on the accretion of facts—visual and otherwise—is a cover for cynicism.

But it is not true of Lindner. His style becomes more acute, his observations more scathing by means of the broad common dialect he is parodying. The facts he records are never left intact, but are milled in a mind which has not forgotten past experiences and knows how to hint at parallels; knows, in other words, where the moral strength of his art lies.

Plate 31.
NUMBER 5. 1961.
Watercolor, 29 × 23″. Collection
Mr. and Mrs. Herman Elkon,
New York

As much as he identifies with New York, and American mores, Lindner fortunately retains a residue of his European experience. It is probably the strangeness of the mingled traditions which gives his work its strength and sharp identity and which has impressed so many younger American artists.

One of them, Robert Indiana, saw Lindner's work in 1954, the year he arrived in New York, and has been a devotee ever since. Indiana reflects on Lindner's position vis-à-vis American art: "What with Mad King Ludwig himself sitting there in the middle of his most famous canvas—confronting Mr. Steinberg across a lady not exactly corseted in the most cuddly American bra—I suppose I did think of Lindner as a bridge between European Expressionism and a very sophisticated American Social Comment. Napoleon and Bach are not even Sacco and Vanzetti. Now, given the buxom, brazen B-girls of his 60s work, I think he has moved from a European to an American feeling. I know his inspiration is from Broadway and 42nd, not Soho, the Champs Élysées, nor the Via Veneto."[30]

Despite the American feeling in the recent work, Indiana concludes that Lindner is nevertheless "inescapably, inevitably International."

This international quality is almost always sensed in his work, even the most American works of the mid-1960s. It is clear and readable, for instance, in one of Lindner's periodic synoptic paintings, the 1961 watercolor *Number 5* (plate 31), in which he draws on the comic-strip tradition. The earliest strips were narrative woodcuts that quite simply told their story from image to image on the same page. In *Number 5*, Lindner recapitulates his story, his pastiche of persistent dreams. Number 1 is the familiar sailor-suited boy with his games, holding his string which will activate the marionette dream. Number 2 is the lush, armored servant girl with her large limbs, designed like a mechanical toy. Number 3 is the same girl slightly evolved, less

mechanical, more frontal, literally and figuratively. She is Lulu as legs and buttons, not as a medieval German warrior. Number 4 is the authority figure, wearing what appears to be a French uniform. And Number 5 is the bourgeois, properly attired, pompous in his bearing, and harboring a lascivious image of a girl within him.

Like *Musical Visit* (plate 94) of the same year, everything takes place in that dark penumbra which indicates a dream picture, and the stiff bourgeois is still Lindner's target. The paintings of 1961 and 1962 weave back and forth in time and Lindner's memory. They are announcing his later swerve to the strictly American and contemporary in small details and tentative compositional schemes.

For instance, later in the 1960s, Lindner shows a pronounced passion for symmetry and mirror illusion. But already in 1962 with *Zauber* (plate 108), Lindner divides his page and has his couple facing each other.

Then, in his more recent works, Lindner has emphasized the mask character of the human face. His masks are inventive: they are the strange colored shadows around his girls' eyes, or a replica of a cat's face, or the sunglasses worn by the pimps and customers.

In these earlier essays of 1962 the mask begins to be apparent in the heavy eye make-up on the girls and the sunglasses on the men. There are jazz-age reminiscences, as in *Couple No. 2* (plate 85), and the emergence of the authentic American siren (*Untitled No. 2*, plate 114). There are also examples of the illogical fancies that become more exacerbated as the years go on, as in *Untitled No. 1* (plate 109).

1962 is also the year in which Lindner painted an important version of Ludwig in which Lindner, in his student's cap, stares at him, and Ludwig bears a target on his brow. The target is probably symbolic, as is the use of blue below his face. Lindner believes he may have alluded, in the blue, to Ludwig's drowning.

It is the year of a tiny collage (plate 32) which is a

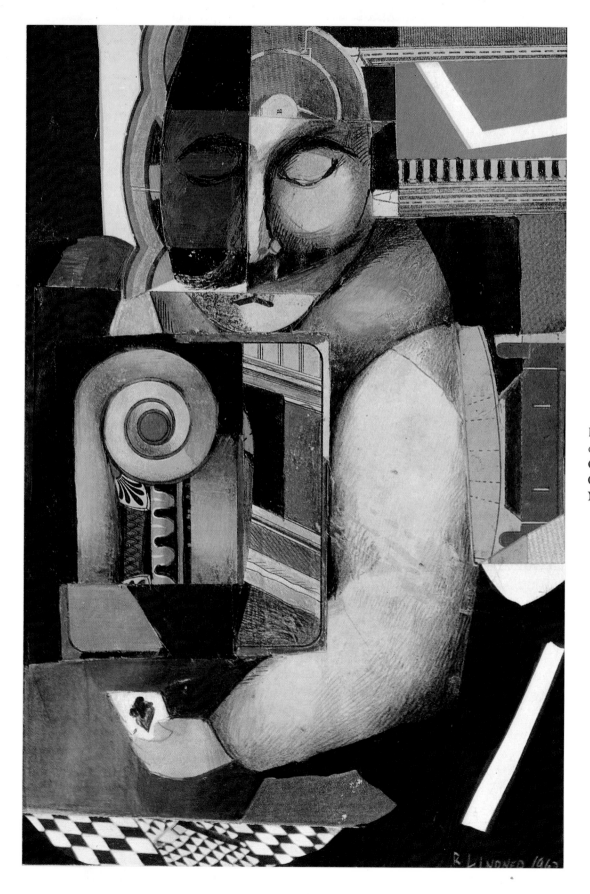

Plate 32.
COLLAGE. 1962.
Oil on canvas and collage, 8 3/4 × 6″.
Collection Mr. and Mrs. Arne H. Ekstrom,
New York

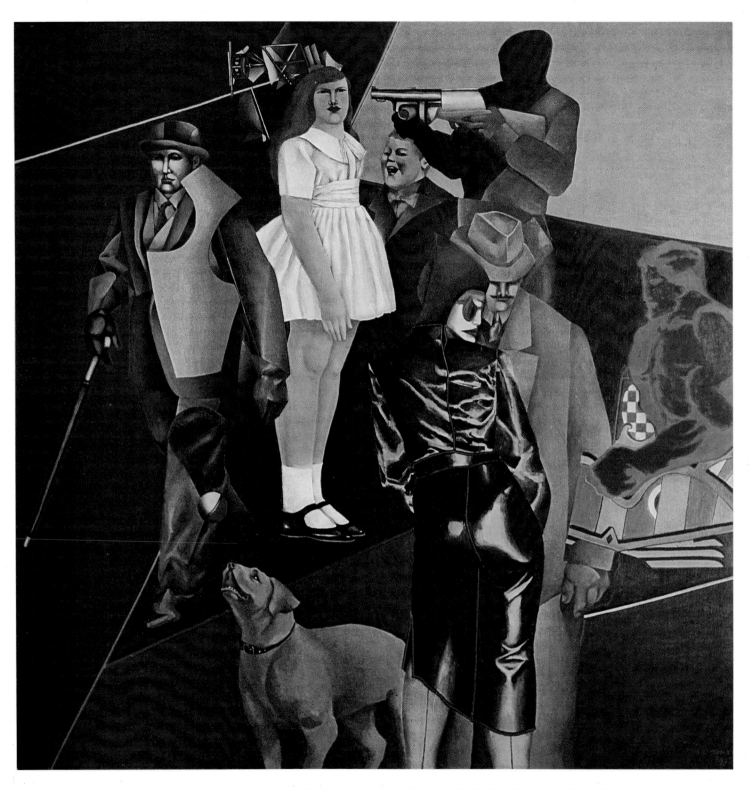

Plate 33. THE STREET. 1963. Oil on canvas, 72×72″. Collection Mr. and Mrs. I. M. Pei, Katonah, New York

synopsis of many past images and techniques. There is a dreamer with his eyes closed. There is a checkerboard, for the games and toys motifs. There are diagrams in the Picabia-Duchamp tradition. There is the keyboard with its musical suggestion. There is a suggestion of paper cut-outs and of theater, and the face is cut in two, suggesting psychological division.

By 1963 Lindner is pretty well set on his course as a bona fide New Yorker. In this year his wanderings in the city, from Times Square to Puerto Rican Harlem and from Macy's to the Lower East Side, begin to register with unmistakable clarity. It is ten years since the initial declaration of independence in *The Meeting* (frontispiece), and Lindner feels wholly assimilated.

Of course, he will never lose his effective strangeness. His early images of New York, like the images of scores of Europeans, are qualified, but never become so familiar as to be taken for granted.

"I had little information about New York when I first came," he says. "None of us knew anything. Just vaguely. Harlem, skyscrapers, Hollywood, and cowboys, that was about it."

The New York he found was more than a little colored by the New York he had once imagined. Its more extravagant and vulgar aspects were what appealed to him, and he now has a nostalgia for that New York.

"It's a shame that the great movie palaces disappear and small dull ones appear. The glamour of Hollywood is disappearing and now New York has a thin European culture. RKO shrinks to a Reade theater. This is a big tragedy for us. The Hollywood climate had chateaus, palaces, dreams that fulfilled the fantasies of bricklayers. All that are left are big trucks, the nearest things to movie palaces. They'll disappear too. Taste invades. The bricklayers have made it."

His nostalgia for another period in New York history is a nostalgia for his own wonder, and perhaps for the freshness of his urban delight. He thinks of New York as cut off from Europe during the war: "It was a magnificent time when Europe was closed. The time of Pollock."

But after the war, the New York garment industry took over Paris, and New York began to feel familiar to him. Its color was draining little by little. Lindner turned to the loudest, the steamiest, the most crowded quarters for consolation.

He found it, at first, on Times Square, where stores stocked girlie magazines and jokes, and whores of both sexes patrolled, looking for the ever ready out-of-town rube. The series of paintings on New York, which continues to this day, takes shape in 1963, and is epitomized in one of his synoptic "machines," *The Street* (plate 33).

We are told immediately by the presence of the leather-dressed, masked woman and the city slicker with his felt hat, that we are now in modern New York. At the same time, the armored Mack the Knife with his cane is a throwback, as is the plump little girl staring out at us. The strange dog reappears, and also the ball suspended in space. But the shadow-boy with his machine gun is clearly in a Times Square shooting gallery, while the cut-out image of a muscle man, painted as though it were projected on a screen, is an allusion to the pulp magazines abundant on The Street. His checkerboard setting refers back again.

A comparison with *The Meeting* is revealing. The inhabitants of The Street are as isolated and frozen as those at the meeting. But they maneuver in a more troubled and less bounded space. They are painted with a sharper and at the same time more generalizing eye. Although the preoccupation with gangsters and underworld ambiance is there (as it was in Brecht's early work) and indicates the romantic European idea of America, there is still a feeling in the materials, such as lethal toys

Plate 34. NUDE ART. 1964. Lithographic poster, $28 \times 20''$

and a comic-strip Tarzan, that Lindner is allegorizing American life, which was certainly impossible for him in 1953.

Forty-second Street emblazoned its rich life on Lindner's imagination, and he quickly converts the last remnants of the dream into a fiercely lit, open-eyed reverie dwelling on the blaring language of signs, insignia, and outlandish costume he finds in the modern New York carnival.

Lulu steps out now as a full-fledged American doll,

swinging her hips provocatively and dominating Lindner's compositions, which become larger and more simple. In *119th Division* (plate 121), of 1963, he brings her forward in two compartments. On the right, painted in harsh colors, with jangling blues placed next to purples, and yellow stockings; with leopard shoes and blouse (recalling the predominance of tiger and leopard motifs in early modern German theater), she strides forward confidently, her armored breasts first.

On the left, she is schematized: a pink lady with the flame insigne from some regiment or other in her belly, and yellow and pink outlines suggesting that she is a sign for a night-club where the 119th Division would be very welcome. Here, Lindner begins his play with signs, which he uses in a quasi-symbolic, quasi-plastic fashion. His use of the extreme close-up, possibly suggested by TV screens or super screens in the great palaces, tells of his emancipation from the watcher stance. He is no longer the schoolboy looking on from a distance. There is no intervention between the looming image on his canvas and the spectator. The direct journalist has won out.

The frankness of sexual mores is reflected in these 1963 paintings not only in the close-up, but in the way Lindner focuses on details: buttons, legs, feet, gauntleted hands, as in *Guarded Woman* (plate 118), and the vagina which appears now undisguised, anatomical and not symbolic.

By 1964 this vocabulary of New York is concretized. Lindner's drawing style is hardened. The neon outlines recur. There are hints of the tatooist's art in some of the works (*Nude Art*, plate 34, for instance), and considerable parody of the contemporary comic-strip style with its heavy black outlines (*Woman*, plate 141) and linear emphasis in general. The girls that appear in the New York City series of 1964 are sharp-nosed, cat-eyed (their make-up is their mask), long-legged and clad in

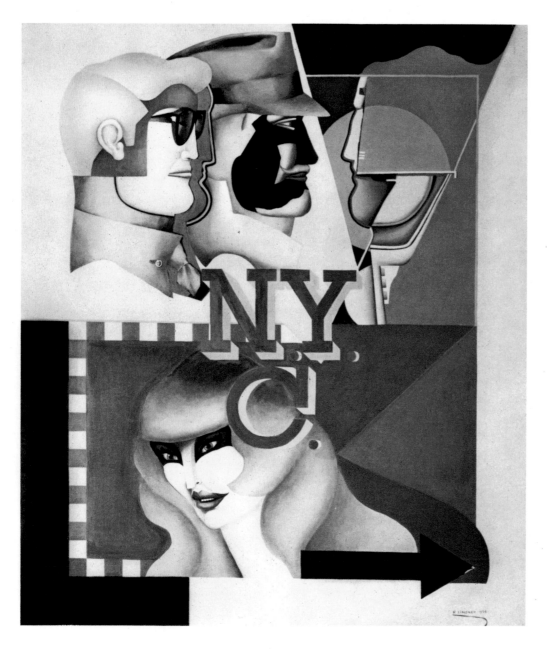

Plate 35.
NEW YORK CITY III. 1964.
Oil on canvas, $70 \times 60''$.
Collection Klaus and Helga Hegewisch,
Hamburg

plastic simulated leather. A kind of salacious heraldry is spelled out in the shields and insignia that appear in these paintings.

The men, on the other hand, are often like mannequins seen in men's hat stores. They are stiff and subordinate. Their felt hats and Dick Tracy profiles do not lend them power (*New York City III*, plate 35). Not even their sunglasses, forming the mask, can make them anything more than foolish appendages to their Amazonian counterparts.

Lindner's attitude toward the male does not change over the years. Even in his conversation, he pokes fun at the male. If he describes a vain woman trying on hats in Saks, he does so with a certain jubilant admiration for her self-absorption. But if he describes men trying on clothes at Brooks Brothers, their wives hovering in the

57

background, he makes them seem ridiculous. Men, he says, go to Brooks Brothers with their wives, but they sneak to Bonwit Teller's alone, to try on their fantasies, which, as he always says, are boys' fantasies.

The men, however, are indispensable to Lindner's erotic motifs, which become more direct in 1964 than ever before. This last version of *Coney Island No. 2*

(plate 130), one of his most startling and powerful paintings, has the man centered like a keyhole. He is a shadow figure with sunglasses—perhaps the new version of the voyeur-dreamer—and the play with the forms of buttons and targets makes him seem like a tailor's dummy.

The girl, leaping into the keyhole or hoop containing her male, is a dynamic opposite to him. Her striped

58

Plate 38.
Portrait photograph
of Lindner taken in 1968
by Evelyn Hofer

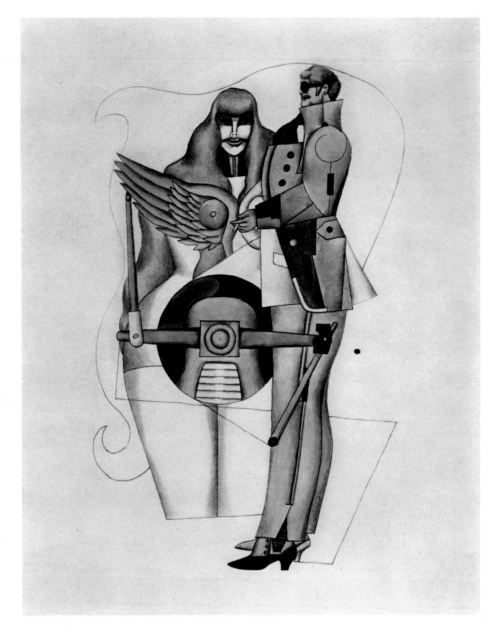

Plate 39.
UNTITLED. 1967.
Watercolor, 21 1/2 × 16 1/2″.
Collection Mr. and Mrs. William Berley,
Merrick, New York

panties and red bra with its roaring panther almost protrude from the picture plane, so tensile are the curving lines.

There is still a mystery lurking in the 1964 *Coney Island* that is completely dissipated in *42nd Street*, a blatant report on Lindner's delight in the New York carnival scene.

This painting is thoroughly frontal. It is a close-up throughout. No dream is possible and no intermediary. In structure it repeats the keyhole, which is an old favorite of Lindner's. But this time the keyhole, coming through as the lighted mirror not unlike the star's dressing-table mirror, is not hiding suggestive mysteries. At its heart is the feline, the tiger. The girls above, doubled as in a mirror, are feline also, their eyes wearing cat make-up, their lips shaped like the cat in *The Meeting*.

The animals in Lindner's paintings have now become largely symbolic, their natures reflected in the masks of his human subjects. The mild cat in *The Meeting* is transformed into a grinning beast in the 1958 *The Scream* (plate 62), and later into a roaring lion. The dog in turn has ceased to be the crossbreed onlooker, and appears rarely now. Instead, his muzzle appears in Goya-esque transformations of human physiognomies.

The shapes produced by keyhole and target and bell outlines suggest mechanical things, such as the proboscis of an automobile—a common pleasure toy of Lindner's characters. The two male faces wear clown make-up and serve merely as heralds of the central drama.

Here Lindner works with emblems, letters, and numbers again, as he will more and more in his paintings. They serve him not only in their plastic definition, which suits the new, hard, glittering style very well, but also as aids in identifying the literary aspects of his themes. He rarely uses signs for their own sake.

There is even a suggestion of orthodox symbolism in certain 1967 watercolors (*Untitled*, plate 39) in which a pair of wings, which could be part of an airman's insignia, are related to the woman in such a way as to suggest the ancient symbol of the harpie. Her foil is a dandy who, because of the current fad for nineteenth-century army uniforms and costumes of a military character, conveniently brings back again yet another Lindner symbol: Napoleon.

This uniformed swell, with his sunglasses and cigarette, stands proudly before the cat-lady, who is rigged up with the old Lindner pulley machine. But it is obvious that he could never pull the switch that would activate the gears. They are unhappily fixed forever in their isolation, their narcissism.

If much of his production in this period centers on courtship and sex on the lower levels, Lindner does not forget his other themes. The authority figures, and hated uniforms, appear now in the guise of New York cops, as in *One Way* (plate 142), where officer number 17 stands facing us, stern and Nazi-like, while above, a trafficking street girl marches imperturbably. It is for us to draw the parallels—to Lindner, the uniformed authority is the same the whole world over. His hatred of the Germans, like Hölderlin's in his famous indictment, is based on their "slavish mentality; their obsequious respect for the outer signs of authority which leads them to such gross insensitivity."[31]

More and more in the recent work, Lindner turns back to the principles enunciated by his immediate predecessors in Germany. More and more he uses the vernacular and the vulgar as an instrument of protest, for as much as he adopts the outer appurtenances of the cool, objective artist of the 1960s, inwardly he reflects exile and a morality.

In fact, the more his work is absorbed by this society, the more surly he becomes. The refinements of the work of the 1950s give way to the harshest techniques and images, as though he were seeking the limits of bourgeois patience. Perhaps he remembers Alwa in Wedekind's *Pandora's Box*, who, in artistic exasperation, says:

"That's the curse that weighs on literature today, that it's much too literary. We know nothing about any problems save those that arise among artists and scholars.... To bring about a rebirth of a genuine vigorous art we should go as much as possible among men who have never read a book in their lives, whose actions are dictated by the simplest animal instincts."

Lindner's way of approaching the simplest animal instincts in his paintings of the mid-1960s is to obliterate the complicated spaces of earlier paintings and to bring his characterizations very close to the picture plane, always taking care that the whole surface is activated. His colors often battle among themselves, being of equal intensity, creating a visual shock. The hermaphroditic vision of the electric guitar player in *Rock-Rock* (plate 170) is keyed to the highest pitch. There is not the shadow of an equivocation, and not the slightest sentiment other than wincing awe displayed.

By crowding everything forward on the picture plane and bringing color to an almost unbearably high pitch, as Lindner does in *Rock-Rock*, in *42nd Street*, and in *Disney Land* (plate 151), he eliminates all intermediary emotions. The stark animal existence is right there on the surface.

Animalism, and its human expression, has long been one of Lindner's favored themes, but in later works, such as *Disney Land*, the romantic metaphor disappears. A sharp-beaked parrot participates, completing the image of human absurdity. The repetition of eyes, along with numbers and letters, underlines the direct equation of animal and human. Where in the 1962 diptych, showing a disrobing woman with a dog, there is still a certain ambivalence of meaning, in the work from 1966 onward animals present themselves quite simply as the equals of humans, neither more nor less interesting.

Unquestionably, Lindner has found the means to express his intense feeling about the city, about New York. Like Brecht, another product of the Bavarian provinces, he can say: "In der Asphaltstadt bin ich Daheim." ("In the asphalt city I am at home.")

In his most recent work, which has become a continuing narrative of his response to New York, Lindner's intense color echoes the color and noise of the city. From the trucks, signs, taxis, and the streets themselves he has developed a kind of visual argot to accompany the mute gestures of the generalized figures in his paintings. Although he generalizes in his paintings when he does his "research," he sharpens his mind's eye by familiarizing himself with specific people. None of his paintings derives from the mass media, which is what distinguishes him from the so-called Pop artists. His images are all based on his personal observations of the people themselves. "I know a Brooklyn face, a Bronx face, a Manhattan face," he says proudly.

That he sets high value upon the process of observation is confirmed by the reminiscence of one of his students, who quotes him as having said that observation is everything. Courses in art school ought not to be given names, he told his students; they should just be called observation.[32]

The student describes one of his methods of training observation: The unclothed model would be posed, and he would say, "Don't draw, look!" After a few minutes, he would ask his students to write, but not draw, their impressions, naming the model, suggesting her temperament, habits, and occupations. Then the whole class, and also the model, would converse for a while, and then—only then—would they begin to draw.

From this account of his classroom approach, it is not difficult to imagine Lindner's method of research as he prowls around New York, sequestering images for future works.

His New York series in the future, he says, will talk of New York's children, young people, middle-aged people, and old people, and all the animals in the city. After all, the Zoo is in the middle of the city. "A lion could be walking around the city. I have heard the lions roaring."

The children are no longer the repulsive prodigies of his early work: "I don't see children any more as I did. I see them as related to Macy's. Children are like grownups: business people. At Woolworth's I see them trying out toys. Being a child is being in a monstrous small business world. But the real children, of course, are over sixty. Everyone who retires becomes a real child."

More and more, Lindner's work moves together into

a total oeuvre with a gloomy allegorical meaning. If he says "Macy's is a symbol of the city, a continuation of the subway," he cryptically presents a point of view that becomes salient in his latest work: The city is the quintessence of human folly and failure. Lindner sees riots, racial problems, the military with the same eye that he sees aging coquettes, movie-ridden secretaries, and truck drivers.

Underneath the banal life he documents hovers the sinister which he long ago recognized in Berlin. Every citizen, he points out, is a secret criminal. "Our secrets are outside the tribal laws. Every woman is raped many times a day. People take away things and put them somewhere out of sight, and that's what they call order."

In the ceaseless tide of human and mechanical traffic, Lindner sees only futility. He often speaks of the trucks in New York. They are transporting things from one end of the city to the other in a kind of senseless ebb and flow, and people are similar. They keep themselves busy with enormous activity, go about importantly on all kinds of errands that Lindner calls "serious nonsense," but they are all caught in the same brief trap between birth and death.

These masked creatures with their foibles painted or draped upon them are really none other than the medieval fools depicted by German woodcut masters in the *Totentanz*. Lindner's dance of death unrolls in the modern metropolis, but it is no less eternal for that.

DORE ASHTON
New York, March, 1968

BIOGRAPHICAL NOTE

Richard Lindner was born in Hamburg, Germany, in 1901. He spent his childhood in Nuremberg, where he first studied music at the Conservatory before enrolling in the Academy of Fine Arts in Munich. In 1928 he spent a year in Berlin, returning to Munich early in 1929 to become art director of a large publishing firm. In 1933 he fled Germany, settling in Paris. He was interned as an alien in 1939, but later joined the French army. He came to the United States in March, 1941, and soon became known as an illustrator for such magazines as *Fortune*, *Harper's Bazaar*, and *Vogue*. In 1952 he gave up illustration and began to teach painting and drawing at Pratt Institute in Brooklyn. He had his first one-man show at the Betty Parsons Gallery, New York, in 1954. In 1965 he resigned from Pratt Institute in order to devote himself solely to his painting.

NOTES

1. Quotation from Lindner. All subsequent quotations, unless otherwise noted, are from the author's discussion with the artist.

2. Letter to Paul Demeny, May 15, 1871, in *Illuminations*, tr. by Louise Varese (New York: New Directions, 1946).

3. *Five Tragedies of Sex by Frank Wedekind*, tr. by Frances Fawcett and Stephen Spender (London: Vision Press, MCMLII).

4. *Ibid.*

5. *L'Art romantique*, III (Paris: Calmann Levy, 1900).

6. *The Twins of Nuremberg*, by Hermann Kesten (New York: L. B. Fischer, 1946).

7. *The Story of Nuremberg*, by Cecil Headam (London: J. M. Dent, 1901).

8. *A Wayfarer in Bavaria*, by Suzanne St. Barbe Baker (New York: Houghton Mifflin, 1931).

9. *Success*, by Lion Feuchtwanger (New York: Literary Guild, 1930).

10. *Doctor Faustus*, by Thomas Mann, tr. by H. T. Lowe-Porter (New York: Knopf, 1948).

11. *Op. cit.*

12. *A Tramp Abroad*, in *The Complete Travel Books of Mark Twain*, II, ed. by Charles Neider (New York: Doubleday, 1967).

13. Jean Cocteau in his preface to Roger Peyrefitte's *The Exile of Capri* (New York: Fleet, 1965).

14. Quoted in *The Story of Nuremberg*, *op. cit.*

15. *Death and the Devil*, in *Five Tragedies of Sex by Frank Wedekind*, *op. cit.*

16. *From Caligari to Hitler*, by Siegfried Kracauer (Princeton University Press, 1947).

17. *Brecht, the Man and His Work*, by Martin Esslin (New York: Doubleday, 1960).

18. Ilse Getz remembers that there were many physically monstrous types, including cretins, in the Nuremberg of her childhood.

19. The Nuremberger's preoccupation with the *Wunderkind* is traditional. The legend of the mysterious Kaspar Hauser, for example, was known to every schoolboy during Lindner's childhood.

20. *Op. cit.*

21. *Americans*, 1963. Catalogue of an exhibition directed by Dorothy Miller.

22. "The Machine Style of Francis Picabia," by William A. Camfield, *The Art Bulletin*, Sept.-Dec., 1966.

23. Quoted by Ernest Schumacher in "Piscator's Political Theatre," in Brecht: *A Collection of Critical Essays*, ed. by Peter Demetz (New Jersey: Prentice-Hall, 1962).

24. *The Theatre of the Bauhaus*, ed. by Walter Gropius (Middletown: Wesleyan, 1961).

25. *Ibid*.

26. Ilya Ehrenburg, in *Men, Years—Life* (London: Macgibbon & Kee, 1963).

27. The firm of Knorr & Hirth published many leading writers, including Thomas Mann, and also published newspapers and magazines resembling *Life*.

28. *Op. cit.*

29. *Op. cit.*

30. Letter to the author, summer, 1967.

31. In *Hyperion*, an epistolary novel about the Greek struggle with the Turks in 1770.

32. Notes from Terry Schutté, a former student.

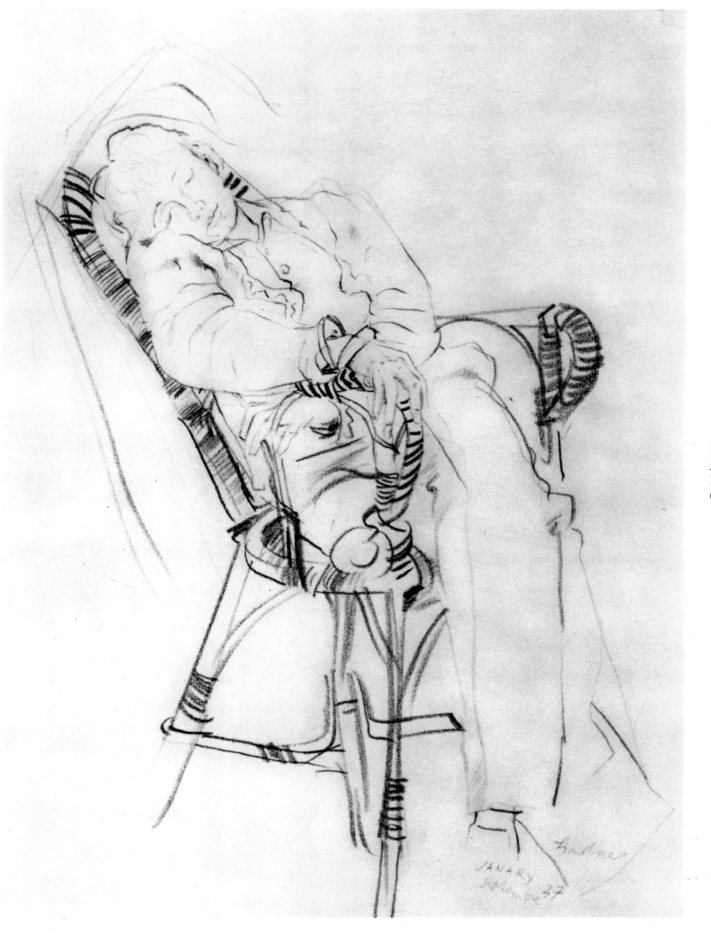

Plate 40.
JACQUELINE ASLEEP. 1937.
Pencil, 14 1/4 × 10″.
Collection the artist

Plate 41.
HEAD. 1948.
Gouache and collage, 14 × 10″.
Collection Wilder Green, New York

Plate 42.
ORTRAIT OF MARCEL PROUST. 1950.
Oil on canvas, 28 × 24″.
lection Mr. and Mrs. Arne H. Ekstrom,
New York

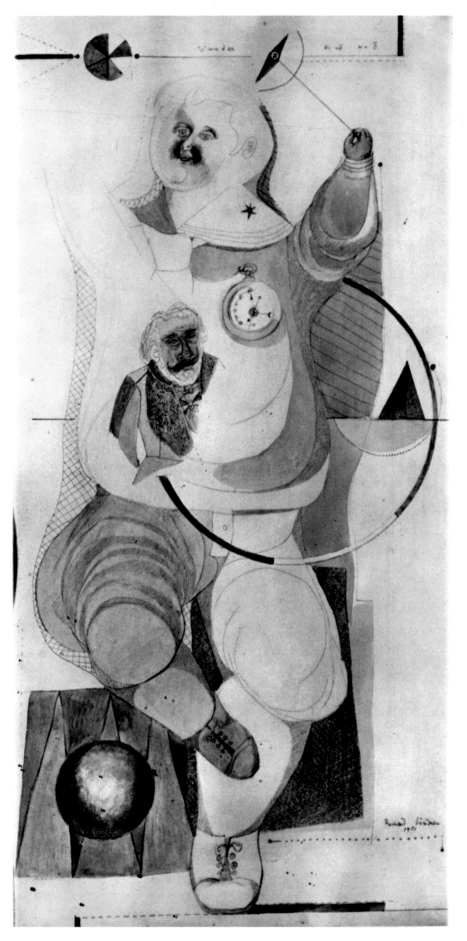

Plate 43.
WUNDER KIND NO. X. 1951.
Watercolor and pencil, 26 1/4 × 13″.
Collection Ingeborg Wiener-ten Haeff,
New York

Plate 44.
THE GAMBLER. 1951.
Oil on canvas, 30 × 26″.
Collection Saul Steinberg,
New York

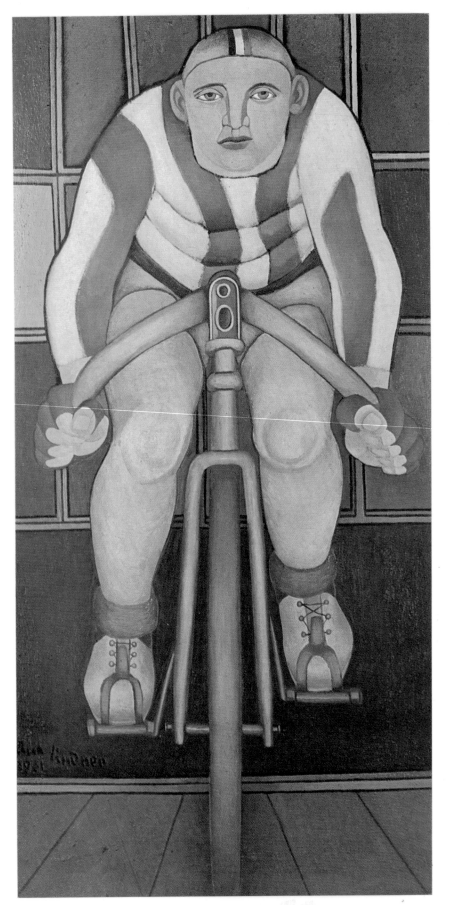

Plate 45.
CYCLIST. 1951.
Oil on canvas, 40×20″.
Collection B. C. Holland Gallery,
Chicago, Illinois

Plate 46.
THE CHILD'S DREAM. 1952.
Oil on canvas, 49 3/4 × 30".
The Whitney Museum of American Art,
New York. Gift of
Mr. and Mrs. Theodore V. Marsters

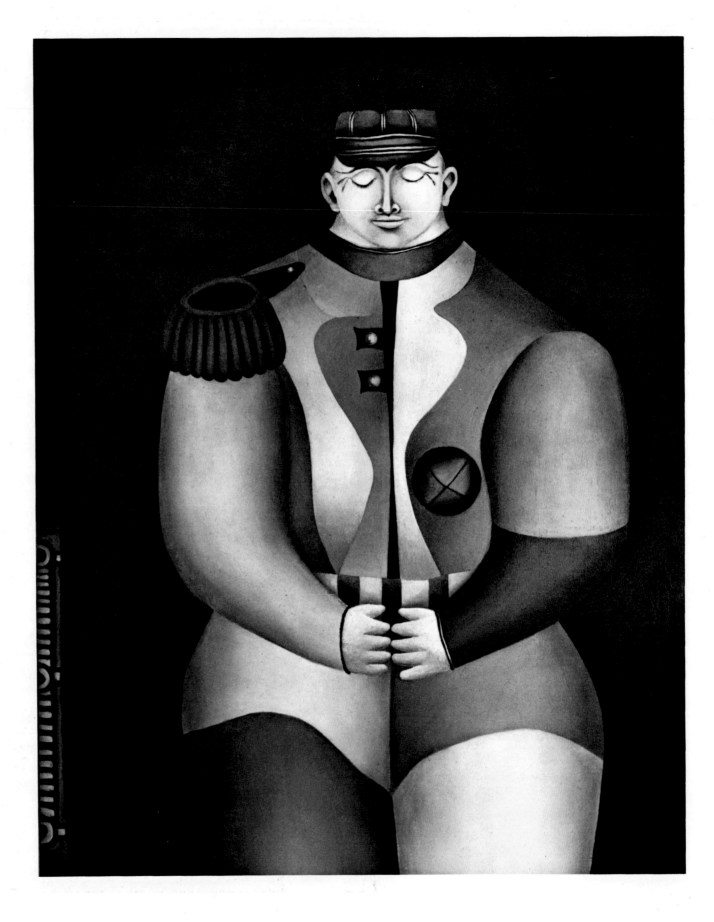

Plate 47.
THE JUGGLER. 1953.
Oil on canvas, 50 × 40″.
Collection Mr. and Mrs. Donald F. Morris,
Detroit, Michigan.
Courtesy Donald Morris Gallery, Detroit

Plate 48.
THE VISITOR. 1953.
Oil on canvas, 50 × 30″.
Collection Miss Helen Mary Harding,
New York

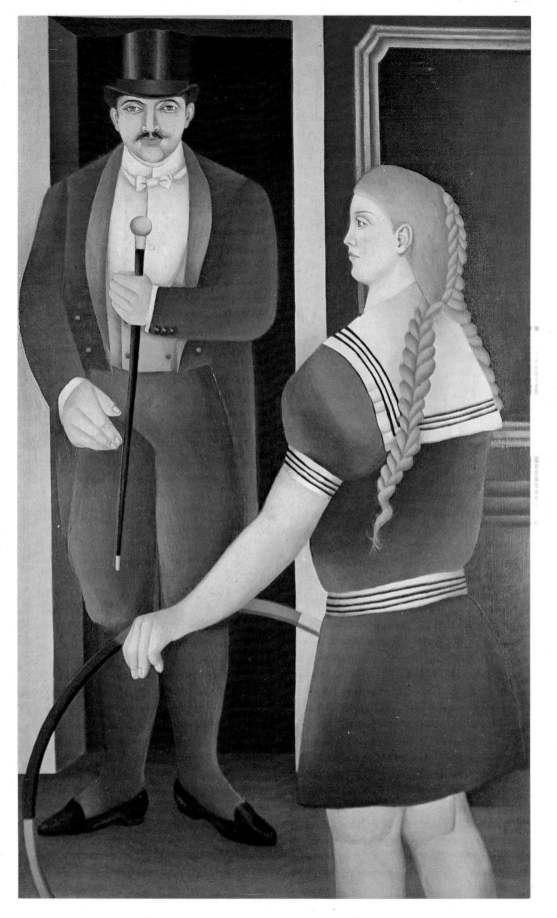

Plate 49.
ACADEMICIAN. 1954.
Oil pastel, pen and ink,
28 1/4 × 22 1/8″.
Collection Dr. and Mrs.
Hans Lehfeldt, New York

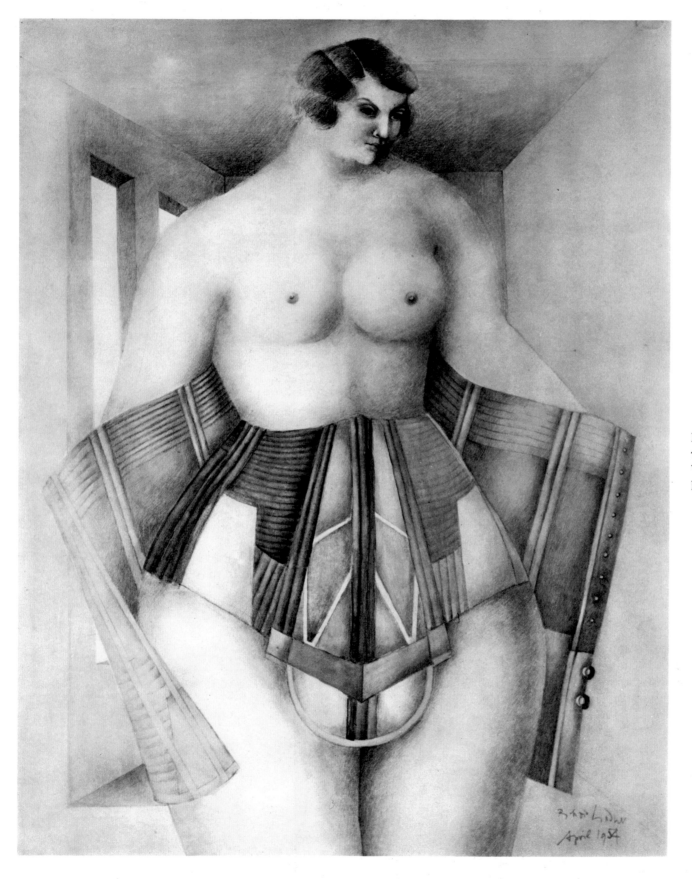

Plate 50.
THE CORSET. 1954.
Watercolor, 29 × 23″.
Private collection

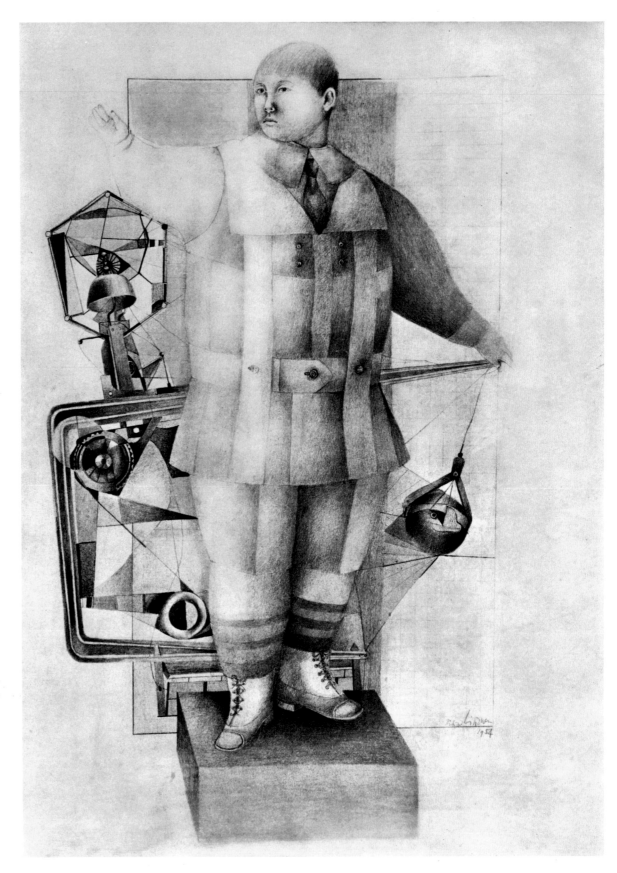

Plate 51.
UNTITLED. 1954.
Pencil and crayon, 25 1/4 × 17 7/8".
Collection Mr. and Mrs. Douglas Auchincloss,
New York

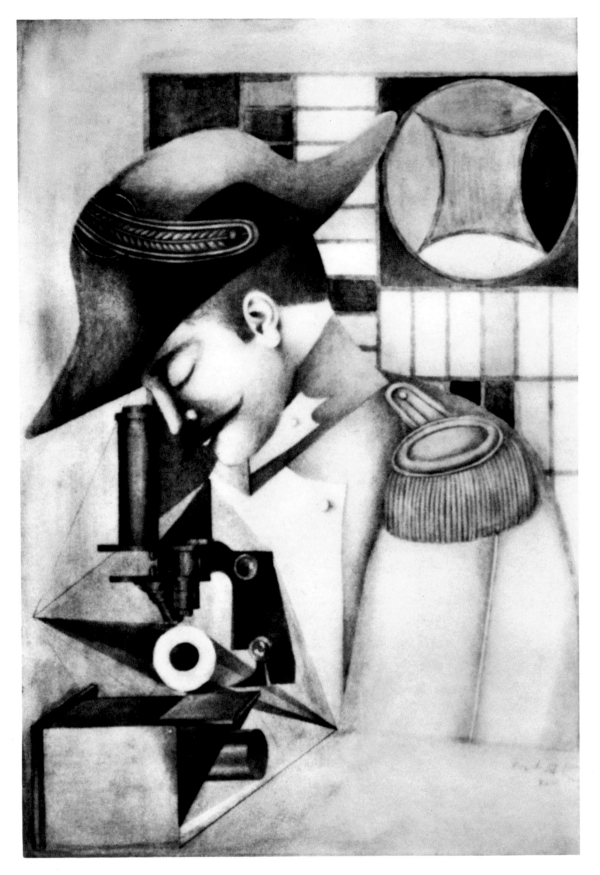

Plate 52.
THE ADMIRAL. 1954.
Watercolor, 25 1/2 × 18".
Collection Union Carbide Corporation

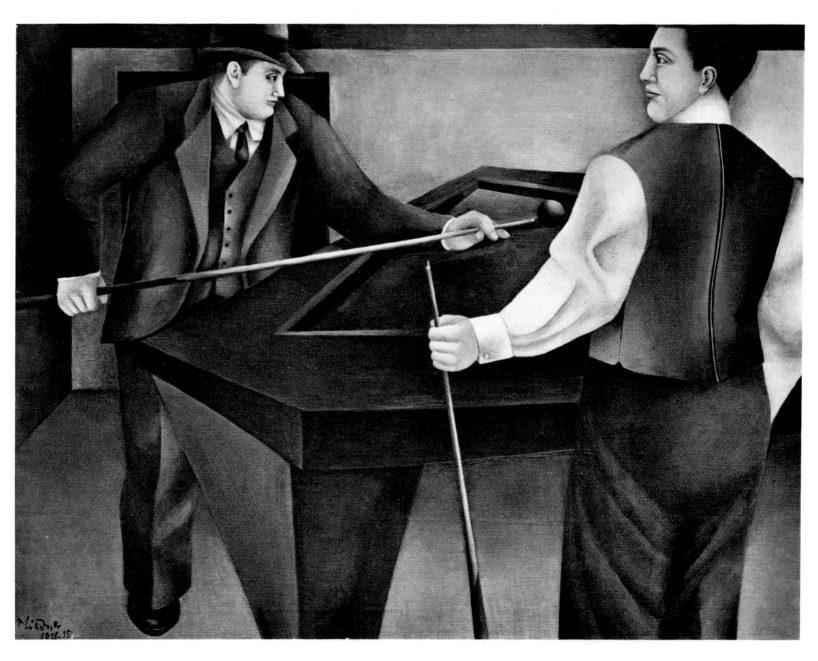

Plate 53. THE BILLIARD. 1954–55. Oil on canvas, 30 × 40″. Collection H. Marc Moyens, Alexandria, Virginia

Plate 54. THE COUPLE. 1955. Oil on canvas, 50 × 59 3/4". Private collection

Plate 55.
BOY. 1955.
Oil on canvas, 38 × 26″.
Cordier & Ekstrom, Inc.,
New York

Plate 56. UNTITLED. 1955. Oil on canvas, 21 × 19″. Collection Ala Damaz, New York

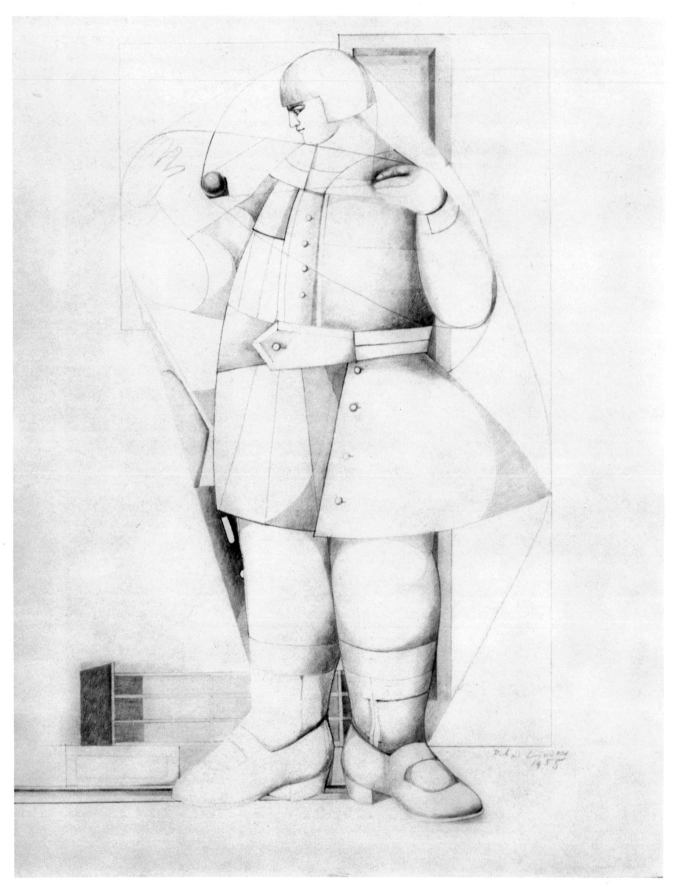

Plate 57.
GIRL. 1955.
Wash and pencil, 28 1/2 × 22 5/8".
Collection Mr. and Mrs.
Harris B. Steinberg, New York

Plate 58.
UNTITLED. 1956.
Oil on canvas, 28 3/8 × 21".
Collection Ingeborg Wiener-ten Haeff,
New York

Plate 59.
DOGS. 1958.
Pencil and watercolor, 7 3/4 × 4 1/2″.
Cordier & Ekstrom, Inc.,
New York

Plate 60. EVENT. 1958. Watercolor, oil, pastel, pen and ink, 13 1/2 × 16 1/2″. Collection Dr. and Mrs. Hans Lehfeldt, New York

Plate 61. UNTITLED. 1958. Pencil, watercolor, and crayon, 5 5/8 × 7 1/2″. Cordier & Ekstrom, Inc., New York

Plate 62. THE SCREAM. 1958.
Oil on canvas, 60 × 40".
Collection Mr. and Mrs. Charles B. Benenson,
Scarsdale, New York

Plate 63.
STRANGER NO. 1. 1958.
Oil on canvas, $50 \times 30''$.
Mr. and Mrs. Herman Elkon,
New York

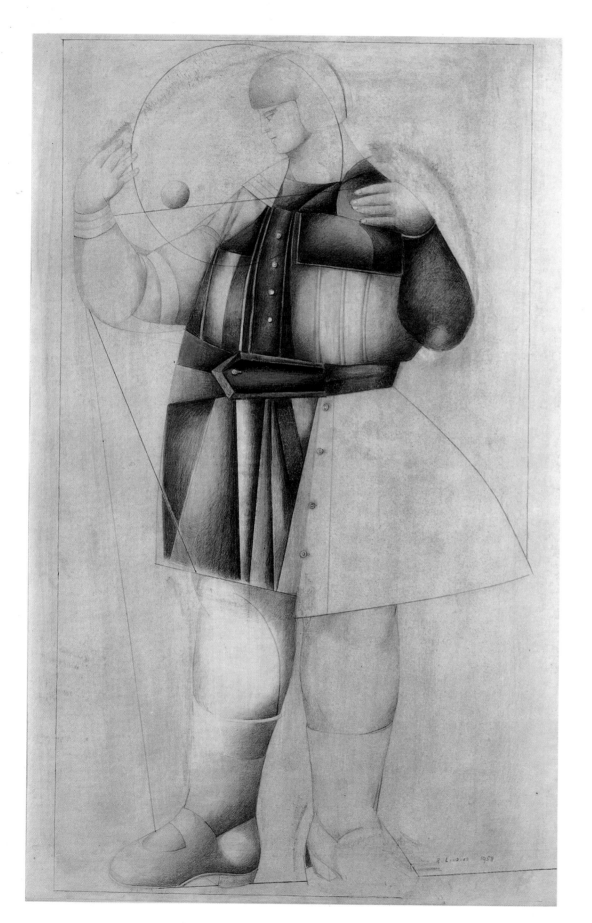

Plate 64.
GIRL. 1958.
Pencil and watercolor, 25 1/2 × 16 1/2".
Collection Mr. and Mrs. Arne H. Ekstrom,
New York

Plate 65.
STRANGER NO. 2. 1958.
Oil on canvas, 60 × 40″.
The Tate Gallery, London

Plate 66.
THE WINDOW. 1958.
Oil on canvas, 52 1/2 × 42 1/2″.
Cordier & Ekstrom, Inc., New York

Plate 67.
THE ENTRY. 1958.
Oil on canvas, 56 × 47".
Collection the artist

Plate 68.
THE BROTHERS *or* HOMAGE TO NUREMBERG.
1958. Oil on canvas, 50 × 40".
Private collection

Plate 69.
P A U S E. 1958–61.
Oil on canvas, $50 \times 35''$.
Cordier & Ekstrom, Inc.,
New York

Plate 70.
NIGHT ACTOR. 1959.
Oil on canvas, 40 × 30″.
Private collection

Plate 71.
UNTITLED. 1959.
Watercolor and ink, 9 × 7 5/8
Cordier & Ekstrom, Inc.,
New York

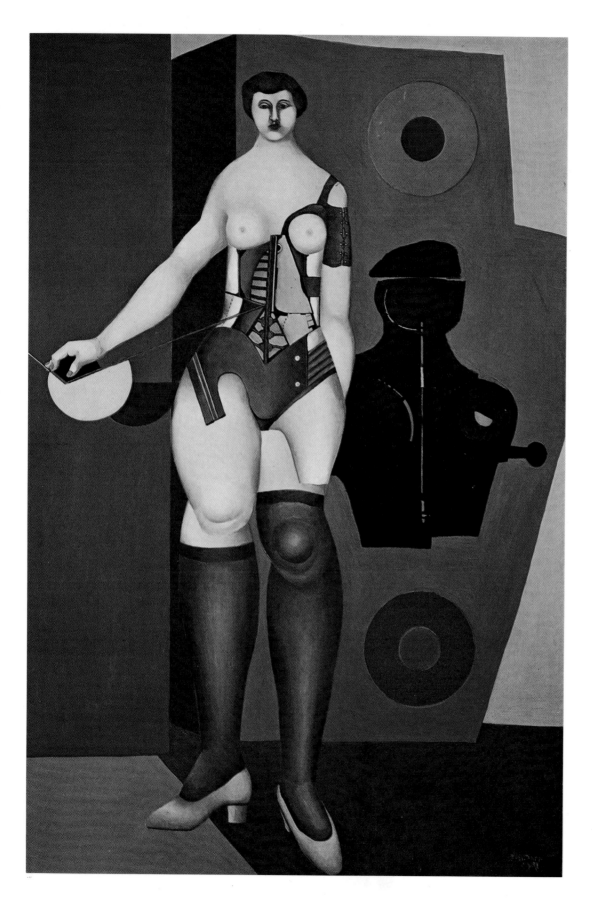

Plate 72.
THE TARGET. 1959.
Oil on canvas, 60 × 40″.
Collection Mr. and Mrs. Joseph R. Shapiro,
Oak Park, Illinois

Plate 73. UNTITLED. 1959. Pencil and crayon, 5 3/4 × 8 3/8″. Cordier & Ekstrom, Inc., New York

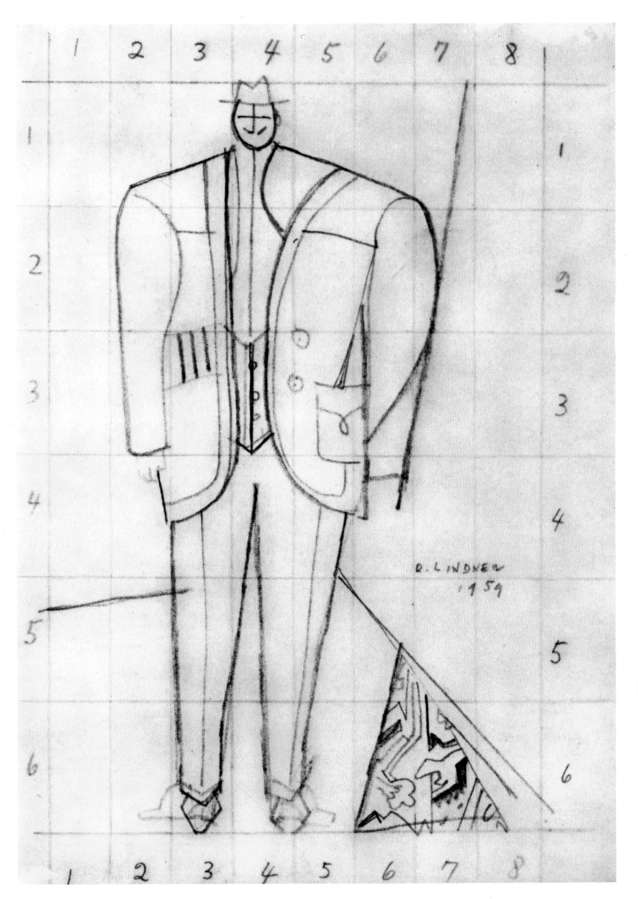

Plate 74.
UNTITLED. 1959.
Pencil, 7×5″.
Cordier & Ekstrom, Inc.,
New York

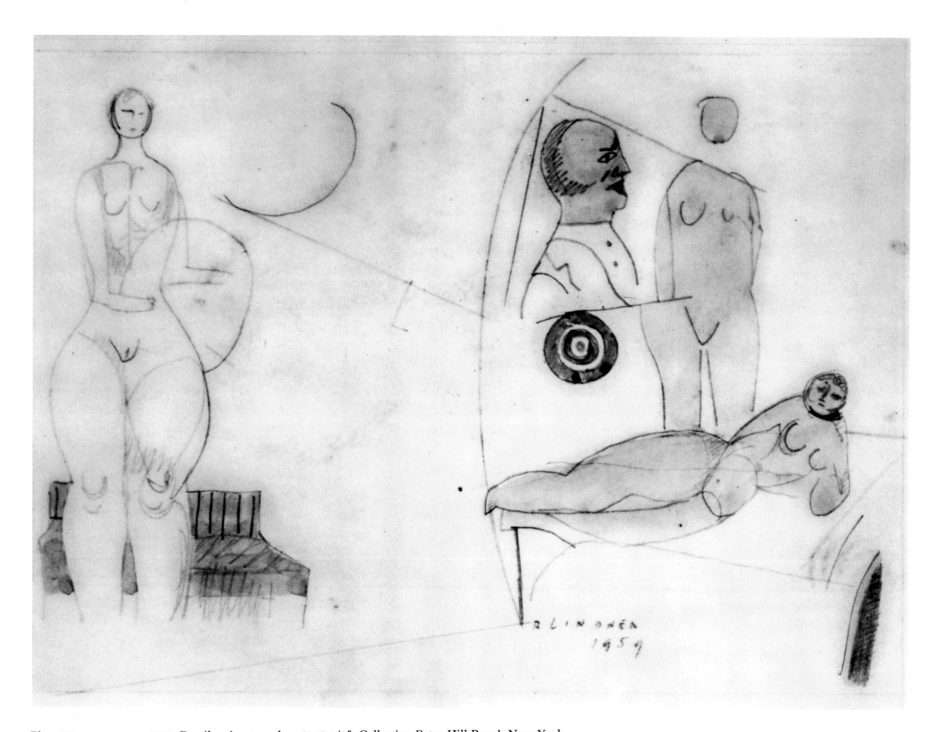

Plate 75. UNTITLED. 1959. Pencil and watercolor, 6 × 8 1/2″. Collection Peter Hill Beard, New York

Plate 76.
UNTITLED. 1959.
Pencil and collage, 5 3/8 × 4 3/8″.
Cordier & Ekstrom, Inc.,
New York

Plate 77.
THE TARGET NO. 1. 1960.
Oil on canvas, 60 × 40″.
Cordier & Ekstrom, Inc.,
New York

Plate 78.
JOHN. 1960.
Oil on canvas, 18 × 12″.
Mrs. René Bouché, New York

Plate 79. UNTITLED. 1960. Pencil, 7 3/4 × 10 1/2″. Collection Peter Hill Beard, New York

Plate 80.
THE KEYBOARD. 1960.
Oil on canvas, 55 × 30″.
Collection Mr. and Mrs. Robert B. Mayer,
Winnetka, Illinois

Plate 81.
UNTITLED. 1960.
Watercolor and pencil, 16 7/8 × 13 7/8".
Cordier & Ekstrom, Inc., New York

Plate 82. UNTITLED. 1960. Ink, watercolor, and crayon, 6 7/8 × 9 1/4″. Cordier & Ekstrom, Inc., New York

Plate 83.
MAN WITH MUSTACHE. 1960.
Pastel, 13 1/2 × 11 3/4″.
Collection Mr. and Mrs. Arne H. Ekstro
New York

Plate 84.
THE RED STAIR. 1961.
Oil on canvas, 50 × 30″.
Collection Mr. and Mrs. Howard Sloan,
New York

Plate 85.
COUPLE NO. 2. 1961.
Crayon, pencil, and ink, 27 3/8 × 17 7/8".
Collection Mr. and Mrs. Harris B. Steinberg,
New York

Plate 86.
THE COUPLE. 1961.
Oil on canvas, 36 × 24″.
Galerie Claude Bernard, Paris

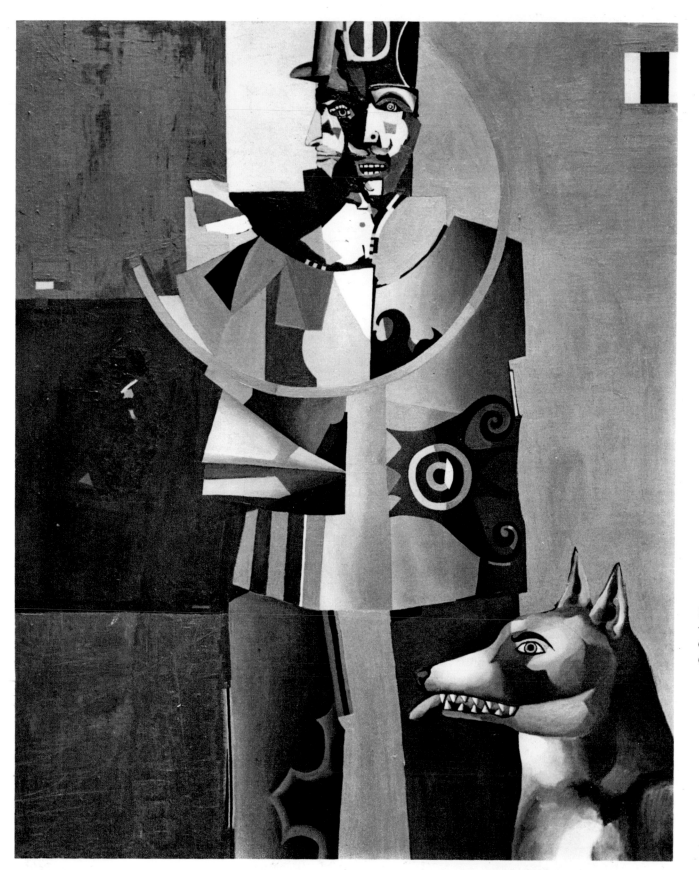

Plate 87.
TWO FACES. 1961.
Oil on canvas, 50 × 40″.
Collection Burdette S. Wright, Jr.

Plate 88.
THE SMOKER. 1961.
Pastel, ink, and gouache, 28 3/4 × 20 7/8".
Collection Dr. and Mrs. Hans Lehfeldt,
New York

Plate 89.
THE TABLE. 1961.
Oil on canvas, 60 × 50″.
Collection Mr. and Mrs. Leonard J. Horwich,
Chicago, Illinois

Plate 90.
CONEY ISLAND. 1961.
Oil on canvas, 60 × 40″.
Noah Goldowsky Gallery, New York

Plate 91.
THE WALK. 1961.
Oil on canvas, 60 × 40″.
Collection Dr. and Mrs. Joseph Gosman,
Toledo, Ohio

Plate 92.
UNTITLED. 1961.
Pencil and crayon, 12 1/4 × 9 1/4".
Collection Peter Hill Beard,
New York

Plate 93. UNTITLED. 1961. Watercolor, pencil, and crayon, 7 × 9″. Cordier & Ekstrom, Inc., New York

Plate 94.
MUSICAL VISIT. 1961.
Oil on canvas, 50 × 40″.
Galerie Claude Bernard, Paris

Plate 95.
UNTITLED. 1961.
Pencil and colored crayon, 7 × 4 1/2″.
Cordier & Ekstrom, Inc.,
New York

Plate 96. UNTITLED. 1961. Pencil, ink, and crayon, 7 3/4 × 9 1/8″. Collection Mrs. S. Allen Guiberson, Dallas, Texas

Plate 97. 1–2. 1962. Oil on canvas, 38 × 48″. The Joseph H. Hirshhorn Collection, New York

Plate 98.
DISCOVERY. 1962.
Oil on canvas, 36 × 28″.
Private collection

Plate 99.
UNTITLED. 1962.
Pencil, 12 × 7 5/8".
Cordier & Ekstrom, Inc., New York

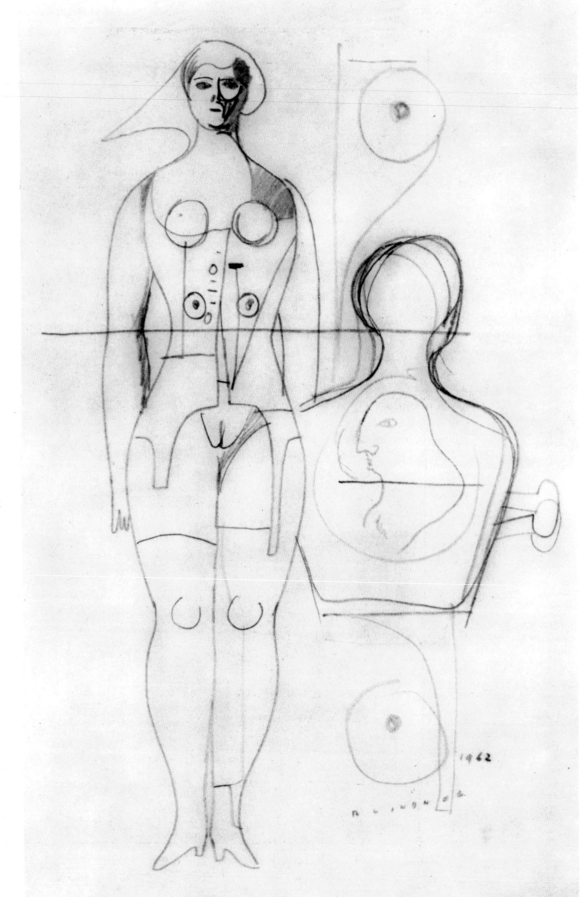

Plate 100.
NAPOLEON STILL LIFE. 1962.
Oil on canvas, 49 1/2 × 39 1/2″.
Collection Mrs. René Bouché,
New York

Plate 101.
UNTITLED. 1962.
Pencil and crayon, 12 1/4 × 9 1/4".
Collection Peter Hill Beard,
New York

Plate 102. UNTITLED. 1962. Watercolor, pencil, and crayon, 6 3/8 × 9 3/4″. Cordier & Ekstrom, Inc., New York

Plate 103.
COLLAGE NO. 2 WITH WIG. 1962.
Collage, 8 1/2 × 5 3/4″.
Collection Mr. and Mrs. Arne H. Ekstrom, New York

Plate 104.
LOUIS II. 1962.
Oil on canvas, 50 × 40″.
Contemporary Collection of
The Cleveland Museum of Art

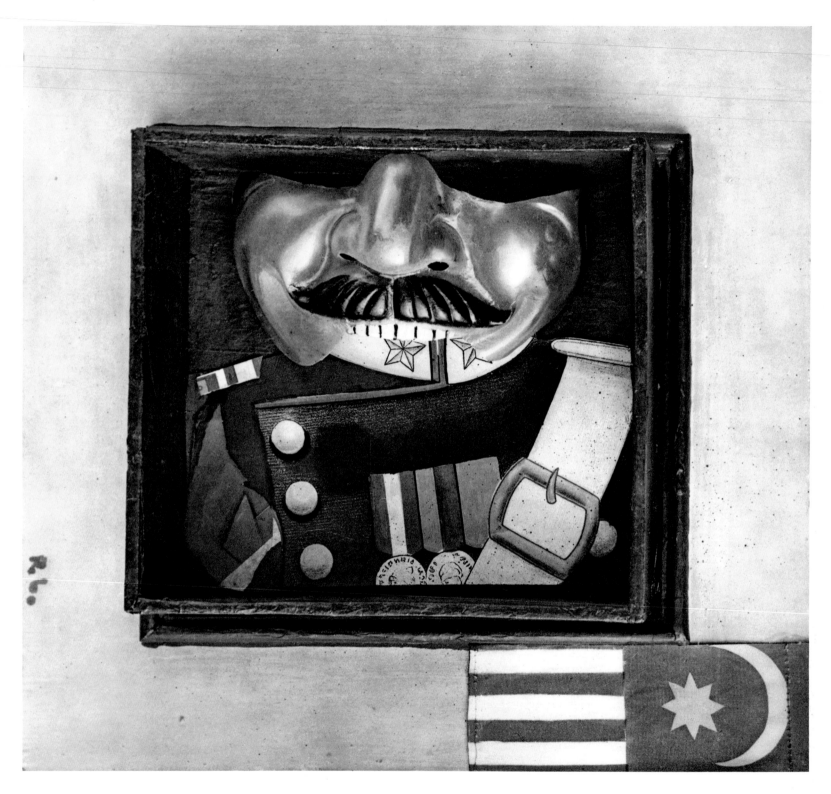

Plate 105. CONSTRUCTION. 1962. Assemblage, plastic mask, printed paper and cloth on painted wood panel, 11 7/8 × 13 × 3 3/4″.
The Museum of Modern Art, New York. Philip Johnson Fund

Plate 106.
UNTITLED. 1962.
Pencil and crayon, 28 1/2 × 22 1/2".
Collection Richard Brown Baker,
New York

Plate 107.
UNTITLED. 1962.
Gouache and crayon, 25 1/8 × 18 3/4″.
Collection Mr. and Mrs. Harris B. Steinberg,
New York

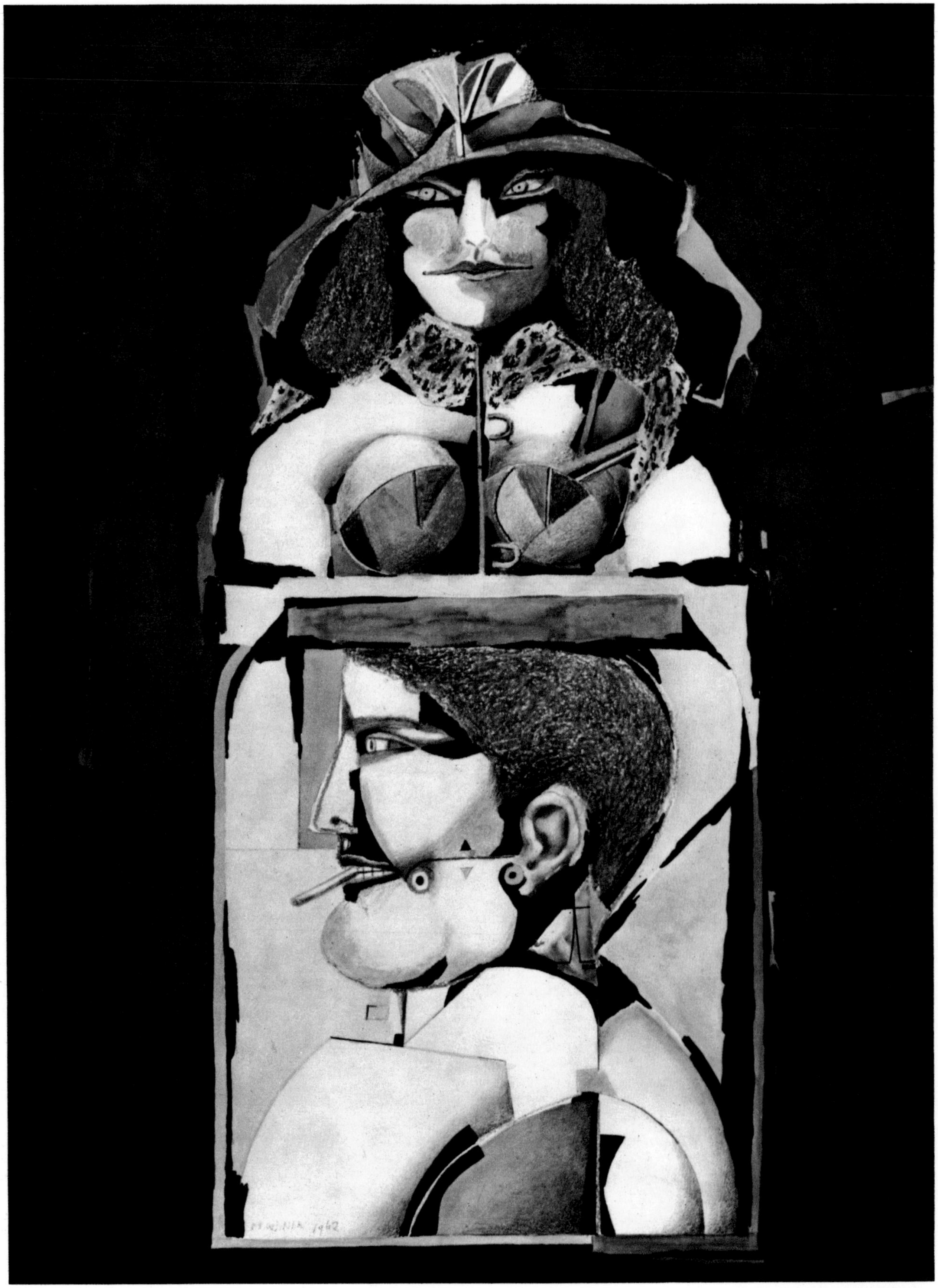

Plate 108.
ZAUBER. 1962.
Oil pastel and crayon, 28 7/8 × 22 3/4".
Collection Mr. and Mrs. Herman Elkon,
New York

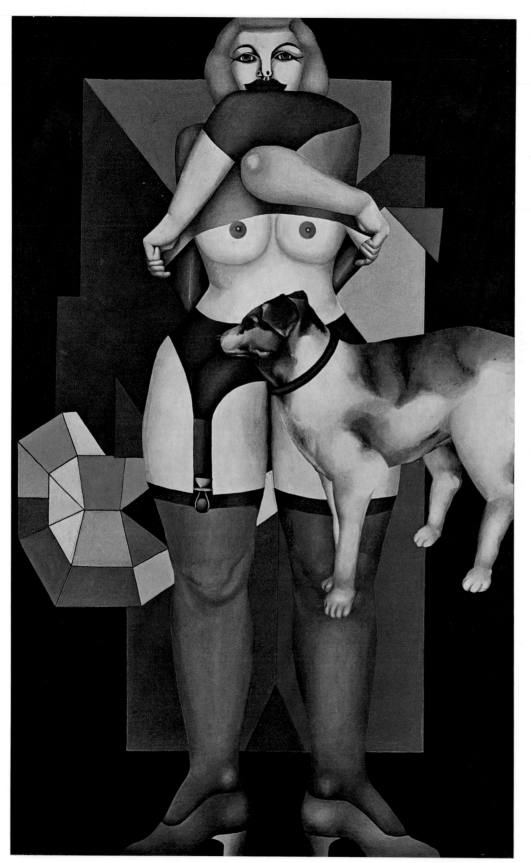

Plate 109.
UNTITLED NO. 1. 1962.
Oil on canvas, $79 \times 50''$.
Collection Mr. and Mrs. Morton G. Neumann,
Chicago, Illinois

Plate 110.
UNTITLED. 1962.
Pencil, red ball-point pen, brush with India ink,
watercolor, and crayon, 29 7/8 × 22 1/4″.
The Art Institute of Chicago.
The Olivia Shaler Swan Fund

Plate 111.
UNTITLED. 1962.
Crayon and pencil, 28 3/4 × 22 3/4".
Collection Mr. and Mrs. Martin Sumers,
Teaneck, New Jersey

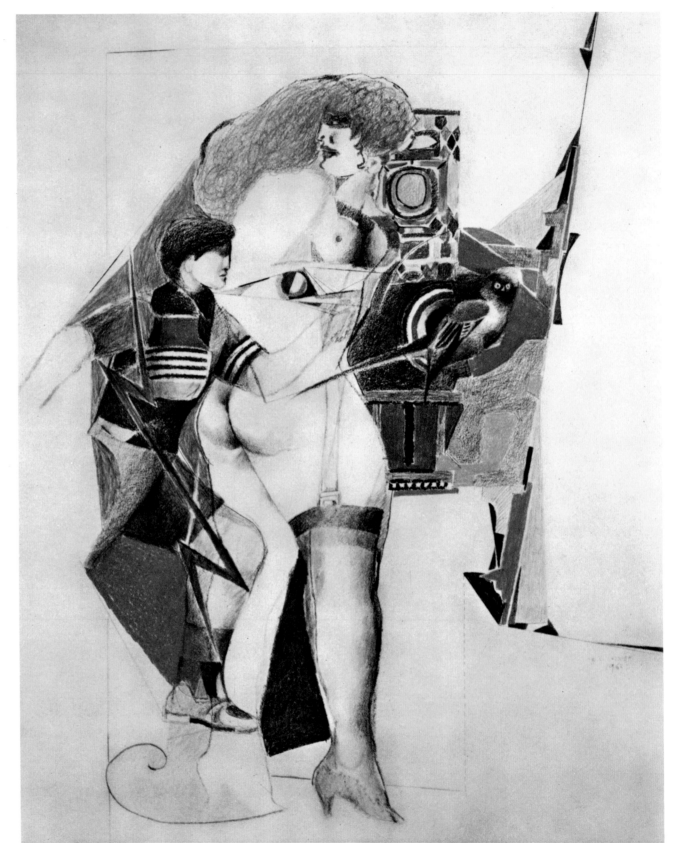

Plate 112. UNTITLED. 1962. Pencil and watercolor, 7 1/2 × 11″. Cordier & Ekstrom, Inc., New York

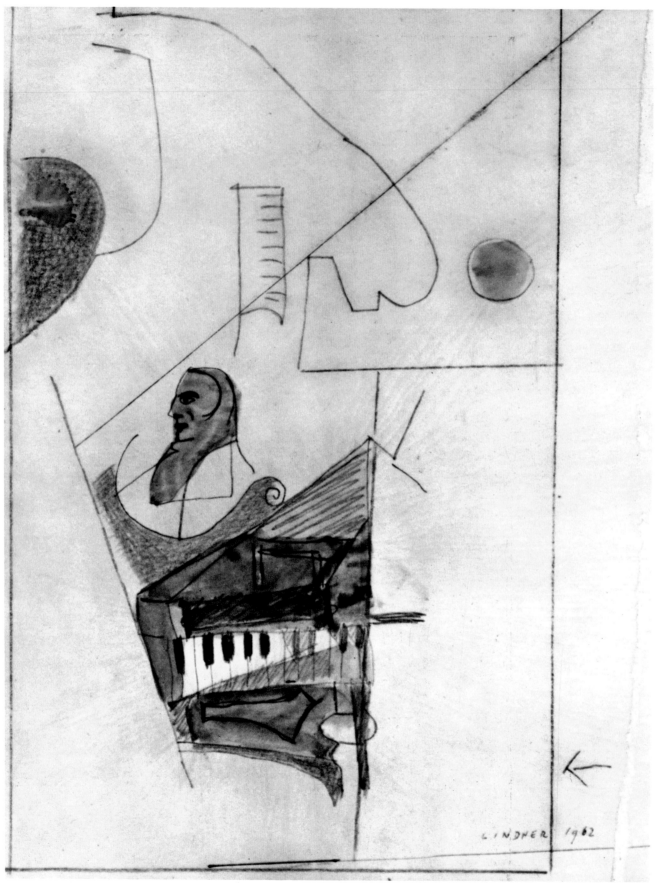

Plate 113.
UNTITLED. 1962.
Watercolor, pencil, and crayon, 9 1/8 × 5
Cordier & Ekstrom, Inc.,
New York

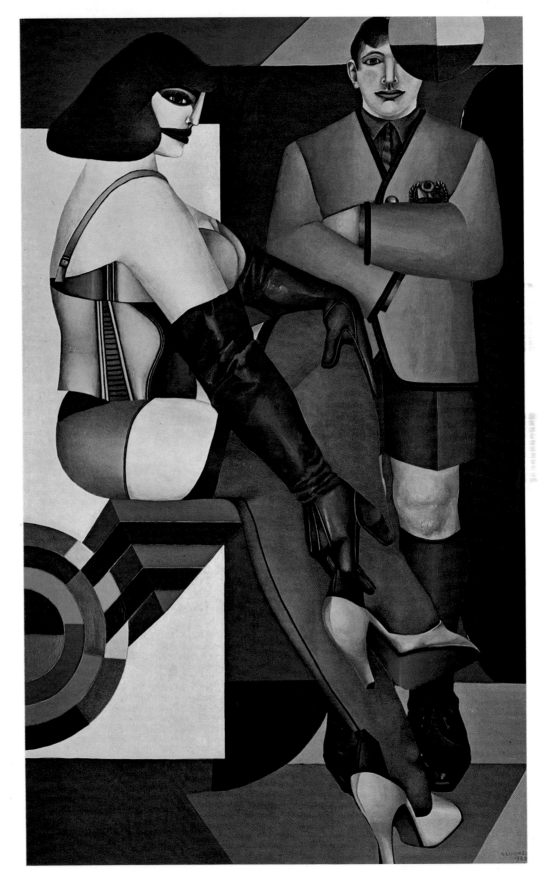

Plate 114.
UNTITLED NO. 2. 1962.
Oil on canvas, 79 × 50″.
Collection A. James Speyer,
Chicago, Illinois

Plate 115.
THE ACTOR. 1963.
Oil on canvas, 60 × 40".
Collection Klaus and Helga Hegewisch,
Hamburg

Plate 116.
CHARLOTTE. 1963.
Watercolor, crayon, and pencil, 21 1/2 × 22 7/8".
The Baltimore Museum of Art, Maryland.
Thomas M. Benesch Memorial Collection

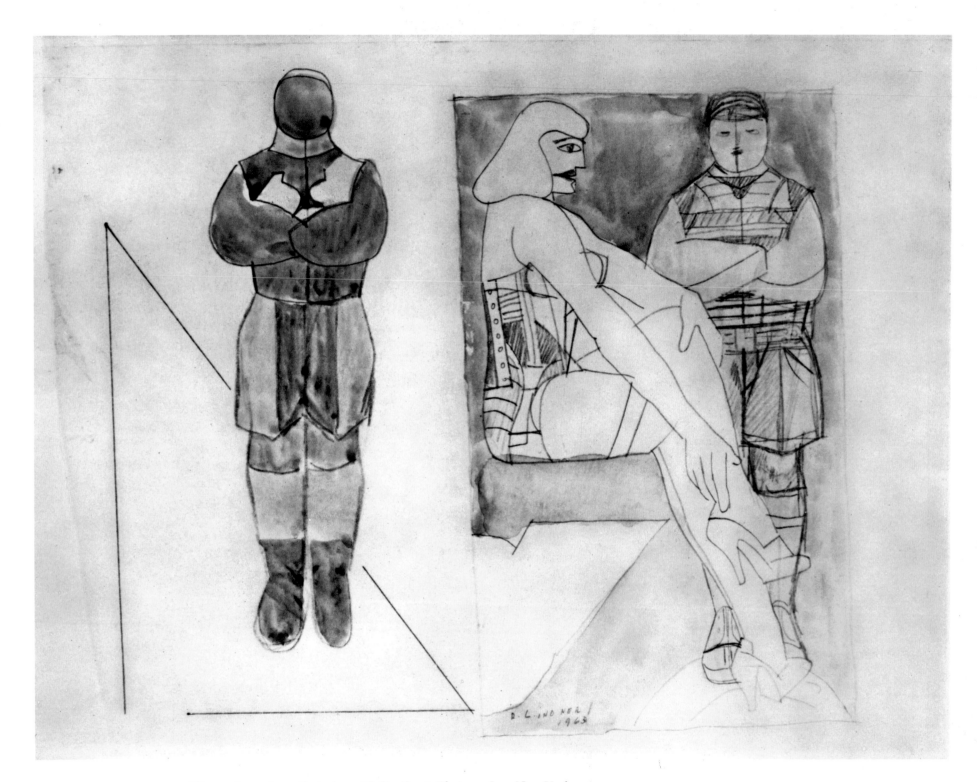

Plate 117. UNTITLED. 1963. Watercolor and pencil, 8 3/4 × 10″. Cordier & Ekstrom, Inc., New York

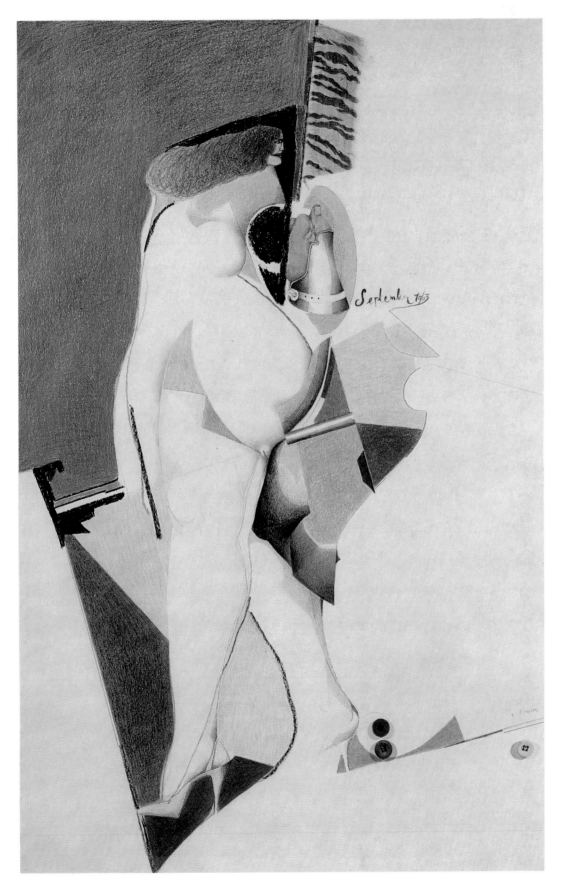

Plate 118.
GUARDED WOMAN. 1963.
Crayon, pencil, and collage, $40 \times 26''$.
Collection Wilder Green,
New York

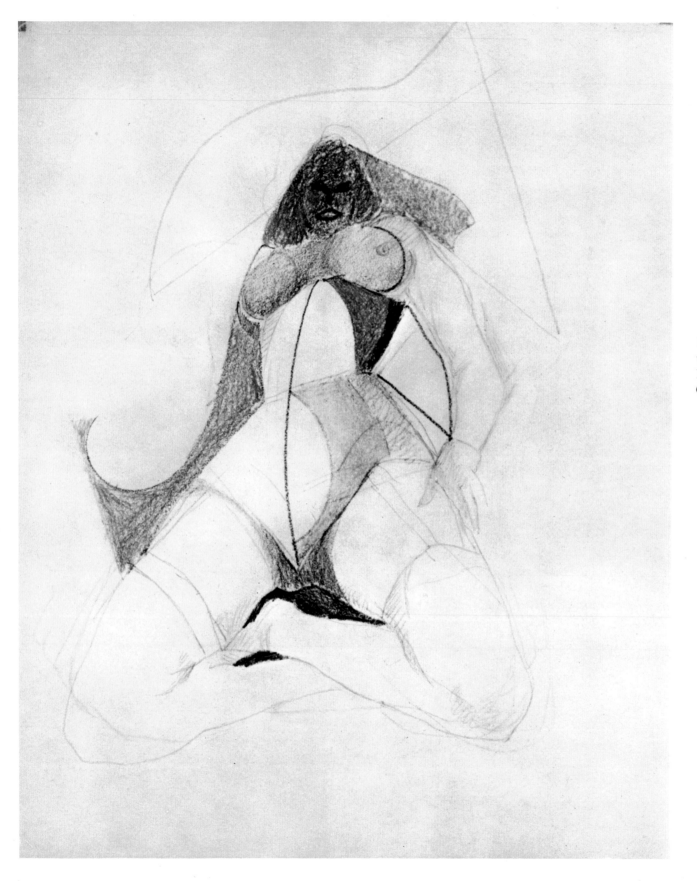

Plate 119.
UNTITLED. 1963.
Pastel, 28 × 23″.
Collection the artist

Plate 120.
THE GAME. 1963.
Pencil, 26 × 18″.
Collection the artist

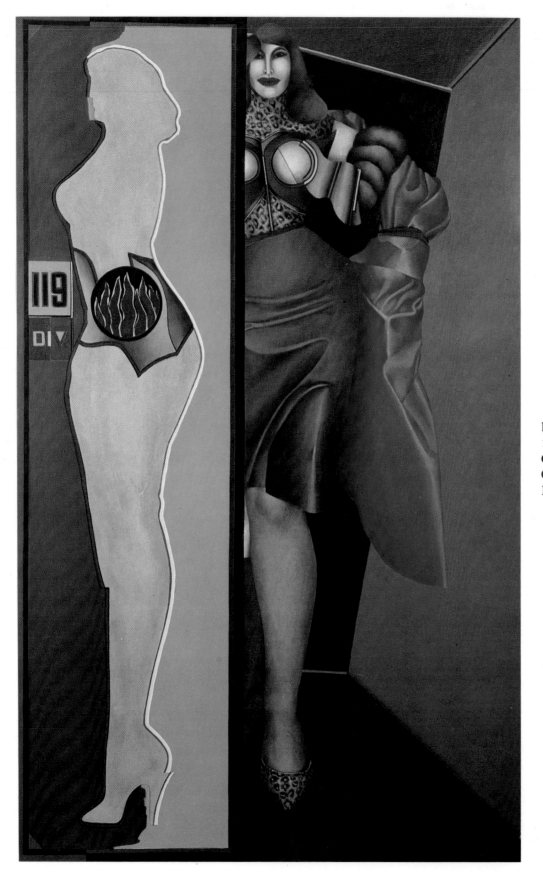

Plate 121.
119TH DIVISION. 1963.
Oil on canvas, 80 × 50".
Collection Walker Art Center,
Minneapolis, Minnesota

Plate 122.
THE COUPLE. 1963.
Colored crayon, 29 × 23 1/8".
Cordier & Ekstrom, Inc.,
New York

Plate 123. UNTITLED. 1963. Pencil, 9 × 12 1/4″. Cordier & Ekstrom, Inc., New York

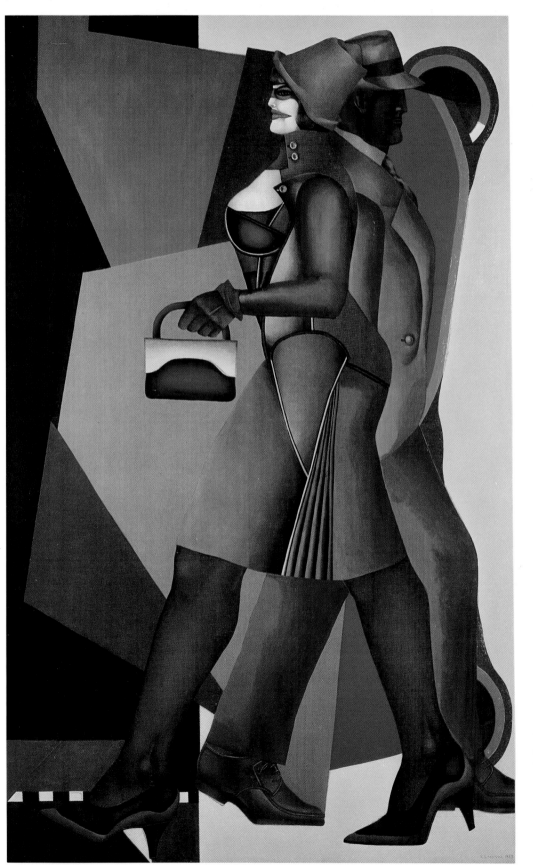

Plate 124.
MOON OVER ALABAMA. 1963.
Oil on canvas, 80 × 40″.
Collection Mr. and Mrs. Charles B. Benenson,
New York

Plate 125.
UNTITLED. 1964.
Watercolor and pencil, 7 3/4 × 4".
Cordier & Ekstrom, Inc.,
New York

Plate 126.
UNTITLED. 1964.
Pencil and watercolor, 6 × 5 5/8".
Cordier & Ekstrom, Inc.,
New York

Plate 127.
THE TARGET. 1964.
Gouache and pencil, 26 × 15″.
Galleria Galatea, Turin

Plate 128. NUDE ART. 1964. Crayon and pencil, 8 × 9 3/4″. Cordier & Ekstrom, Inc., New York

Plate 129.
THE CIRCUIT. 1964.
Watercolor and collage, 40 × 30″.
Collection Mr. and Mrs. Laurence A. Tisch,
New York

Plate 130.
CONEY ISLAND NO. 2. 1964.
Oil on canvas, 70 × 50″.
Private collection

Plate 131.
WOMAN WITH HANDBAG. 1964.
Crayon and gouache, 29 × 23″.
Galerie Claude Bernard, Paris

Plate 132.
PORTRAIT OF S. 1964.
Crayon and gouache, 29 × 23".
Galerie Claude Bernard, Paris

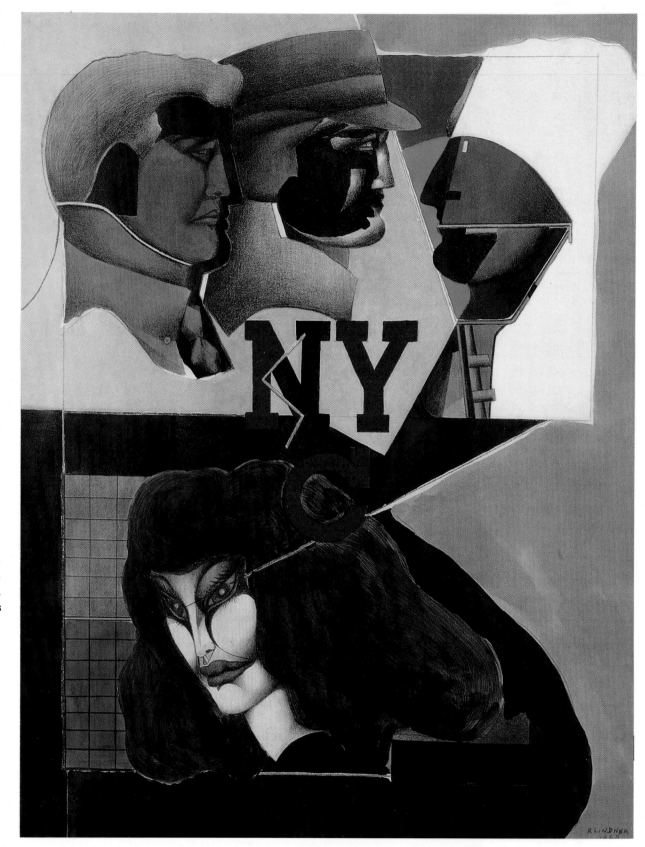

Plate 133.
NEW YORK CITY I. 1964.
Watercolor, crayon, and pencil, 24 5/8 × 19 1/8".
Galerie Claude Bernard, Paris

Plate 134.
STILL LIFE. 1964.
Gouache and collage, 26 3/4 × 21 1/4".
Cordier & Ekstrom, Inc.,
New York

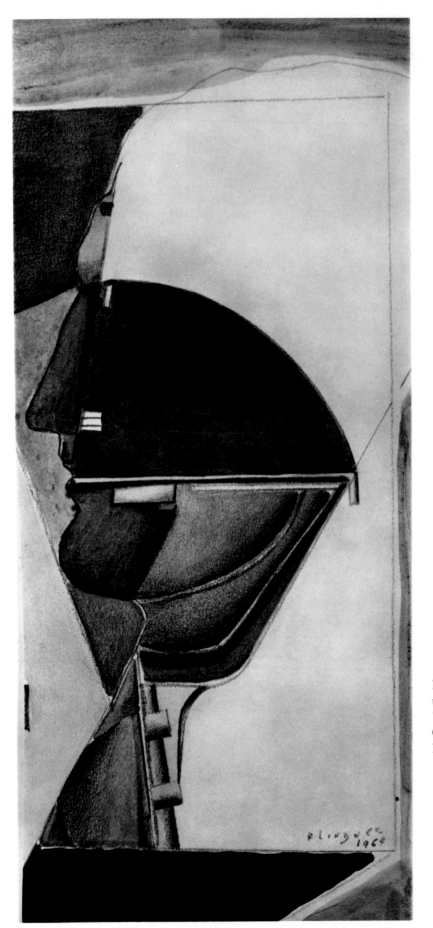

Plate 135.
UNTITLED. 1964.
Watercolor, pencil, and crayon, 12 3/8 × 5 5/8".
Collection Mrs. Robert M. Benjamin,
New York

Plate 136.
NEW YORK CITY II. 1964.
Watercolor and crayon, 29 × 22 3/4″.
Galleria Galatea, Turin

Plate 137. UNTITLED. 1964. Watercolor, pastel, pencil, pen and ink, 5 3/4 × 7 5/8″. Cordier & Ekstrom, Inc., New York

Plate 138. WAITING AND PASSING. 1964. Watercolor and colored crayon, 30×40″. Collection Dr. and Mrs. Judd Marmor, Los Angeles

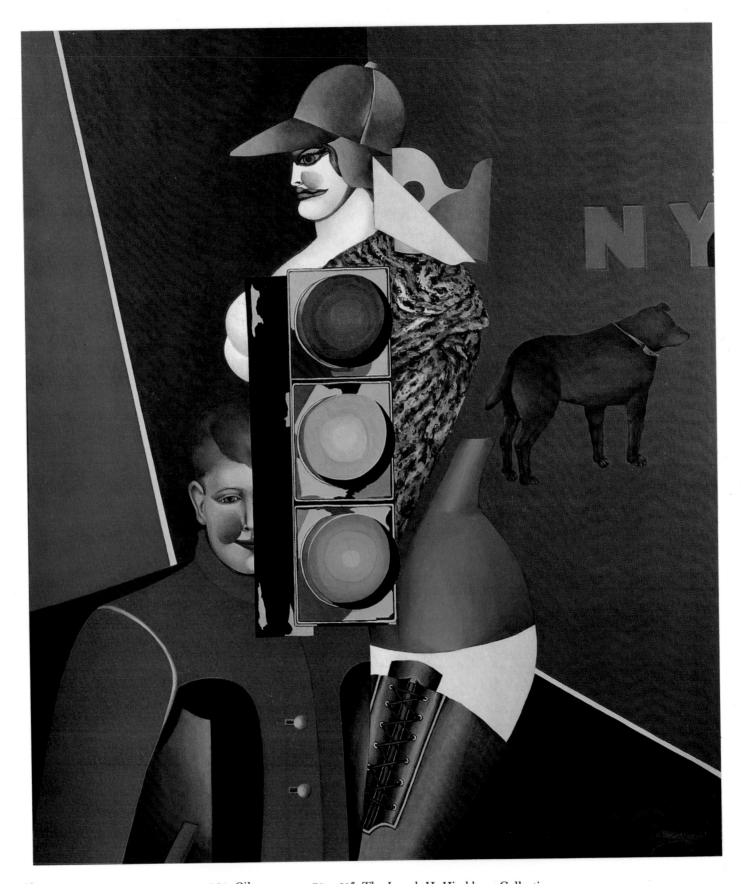

Plate 139. NEW YORK CITY IV. 1964. Oil on canvas, 70×60″. The Joseph H. Hirshhorn Collection

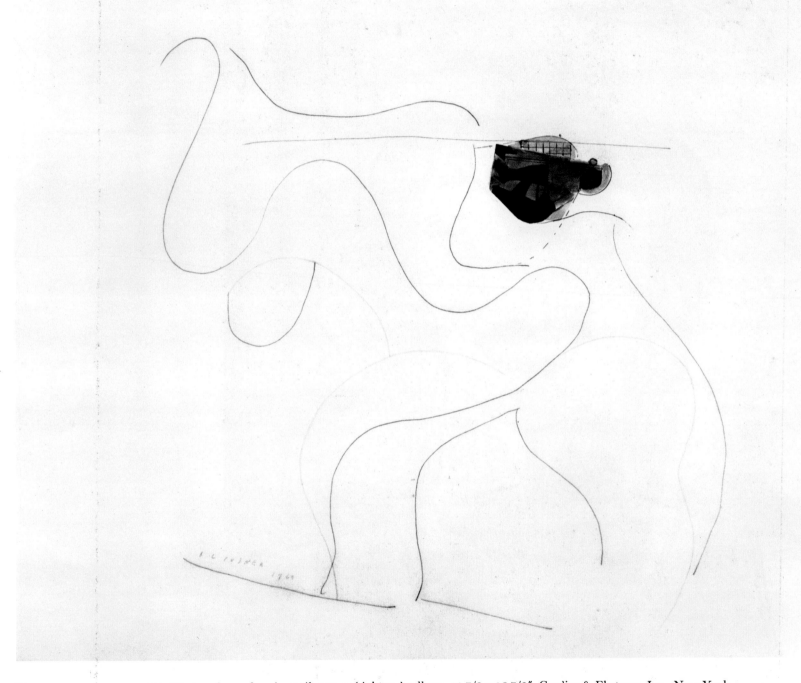

Plate 140. UNTITLED. 1964. Watercolor, colored pencil, pen and ink, and collage, 13 7/8 × 16 7/8″. Cordier & Ekstrom, Inc., New York

Plate 141.
WOMAN. 1964.
Watercolor, 40 × 30″.
Collection Jacques Kaplan,
New York

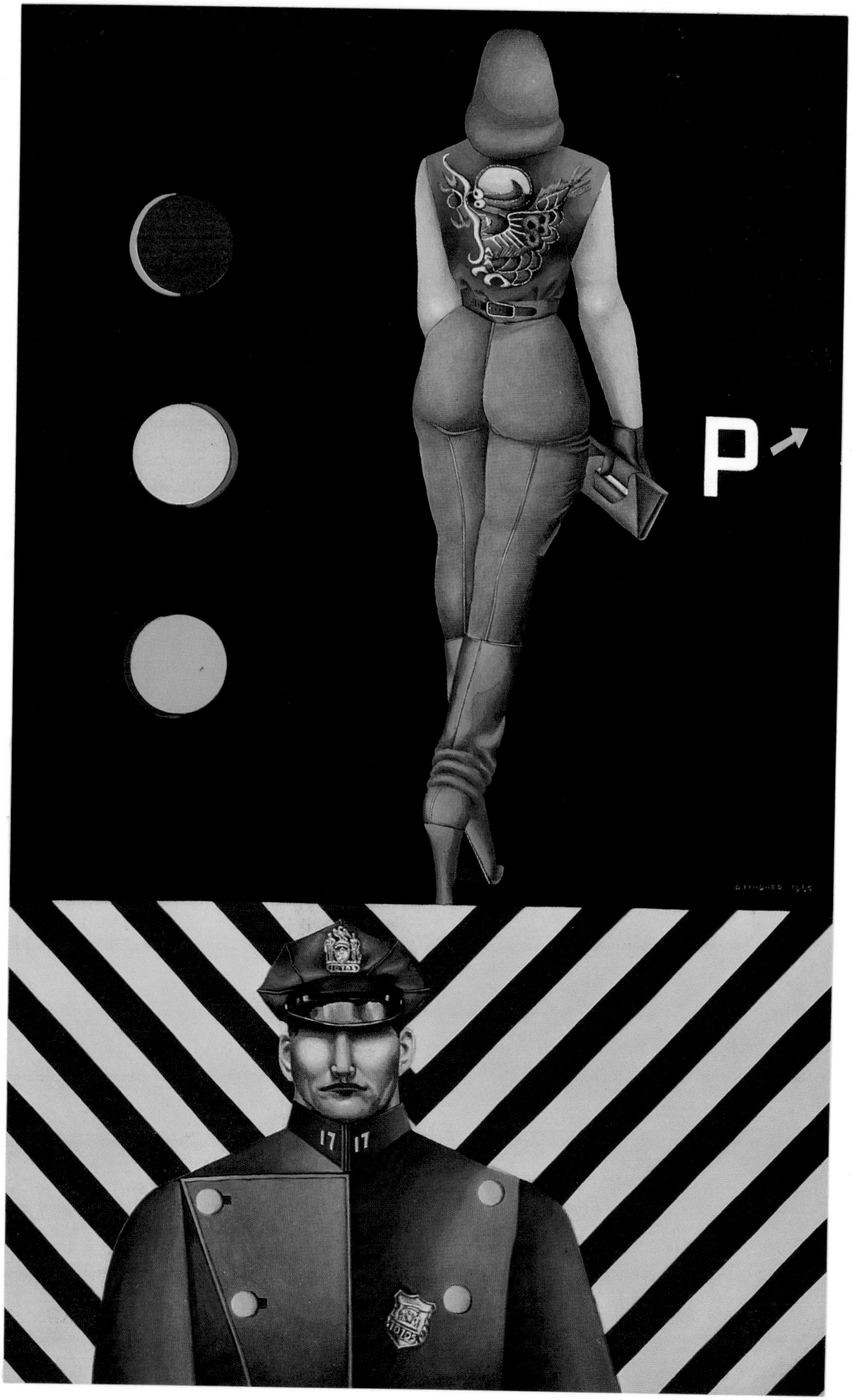

Plate 142.
ONE WAY. 1964.
Oil on canvas, 80 × 50″.
Collection Mr. and Mrs. Laurence A. Tisch,
New York

Plate 143.
42ND STREET. 1964.
Crayon and pencil, 7 5/8 × 6 7/8″.
Cordier & Ekstrom, Inc.,
New York

Plate 144.
42ND STREET. 1964.
Oil on canvas, 70 × 60".
Collection Mrs. S. Allen Guiberson,
Dallas, Texas

Plate 145.
UNTITLED. 1964.
Pencil and crayon, 11 × 7″.
Cordier & Ekstrom, Inc.,
New York

Plate 146.
SKIRT OPEN. 1964.
Watercolor, pencil,
crayon, and collage, 31 3/4 × 23 3/4".
Collection Mrs. Robert M. Benjamin,
New York

Plate 147.
THE CITY. 1964.
Watercolor and collage, 29 × 22 1/2″.
Cordier & Ekstrom, Inc.,
New York

Plate 148.
WEST 48TH STREET. 1964.
Oil on canvas, 70 × 50".
Collection Dr. Max Palevsky,
Santa Monica, California

Plate 149.
HEDDA. 1964.
Pastel, 21 1/2 × 14 5/8".
Collection Hedda Sterne,
New York

Plate 150.
Poster for THE PARIS REVIEW. 1965.
Silkscreen, 28 × 20″

Plate 151.
DISNEY LAND. 1965.
Oil on canvas, 80 × 50″.
The Joan and Lester Avnet Collection

Plate 152.
THE PINK PUSSY CAT. 1965.
Watercolor, crayon, and pencil, 23 × 19″.
Collection Ilse Getz-Danes, New York

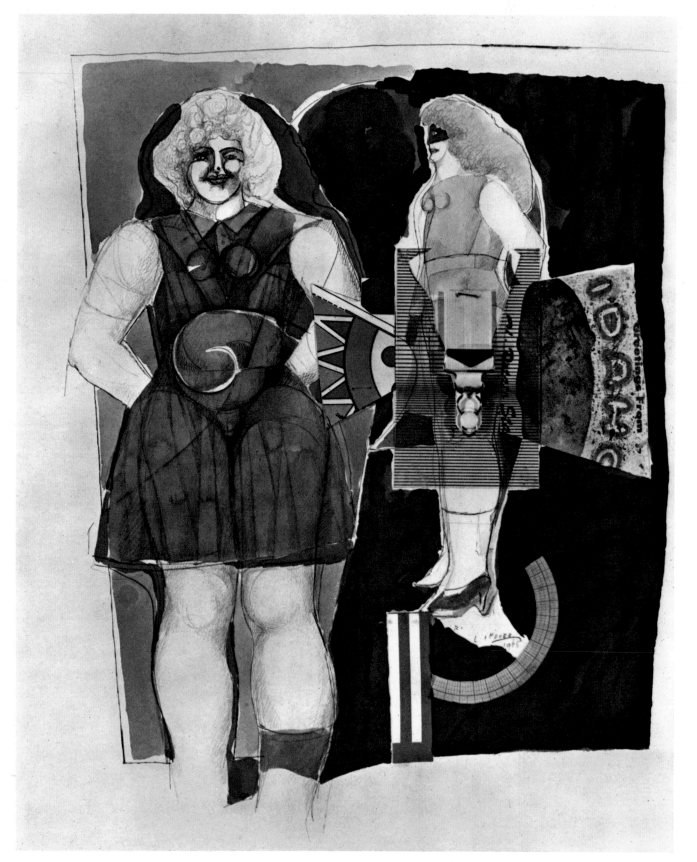

Plate 153.
NUMBER 6. 1965.
Watercolor, ball-point pen,
pencil, and collage, 19 1/8 × 15 1/8″.
Cordier & Ekstrom, Inc.,
New York

Plate 154.
SKETCH. 1965.
Watercolor, ink, ball-point pen,
and pencil, 10 1/8 × 8 1/4″.
Collection Dr. and Mrs. Hans Lehfeldt,
New York

Plate 155.
TO NOMA AND BILL. 1965.
Collage, crayon, and pencil,
19 1/4 × 15 3/8".
Private collection, New York

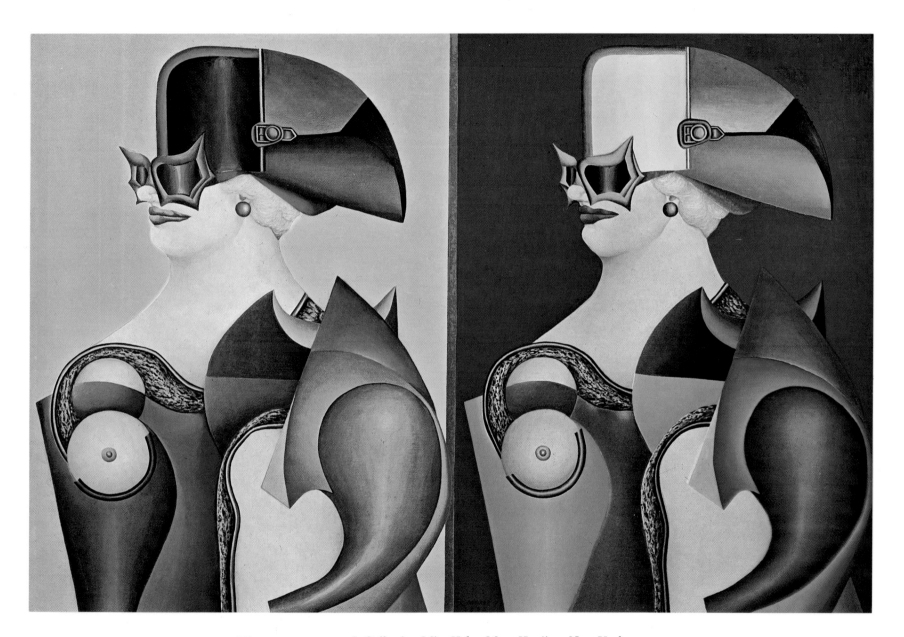

Plate 156. DOUBLE PORTRAIT. 1965. Oil on canvas, 40 × 60″. Collection Miss Helen Mary Harding, New York

Plate 157.
THE PINK PUSSY CAT. 1965.
Oil pastel and ink, 17 5/8 × 9 1/2".
Cordier & Ekstrom, Inc., New York

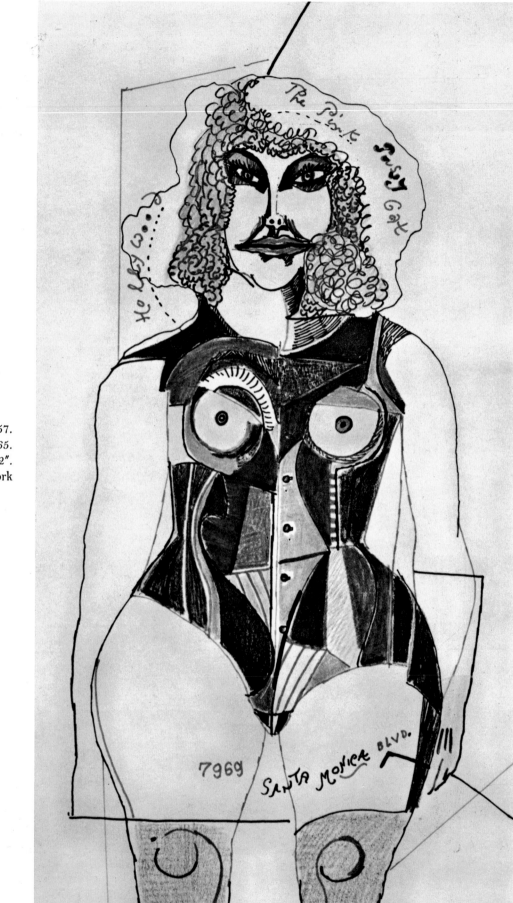

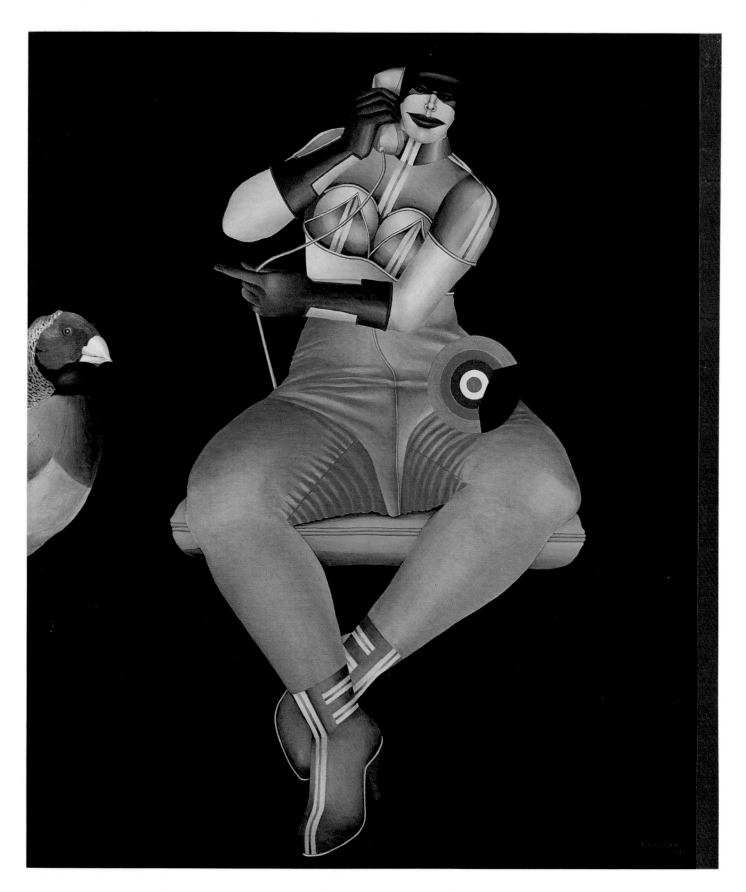

Plate 158. HELLO. 1966. Oil on canvas, 70 × 60″. Harry N. Abrams Family Collection, New York

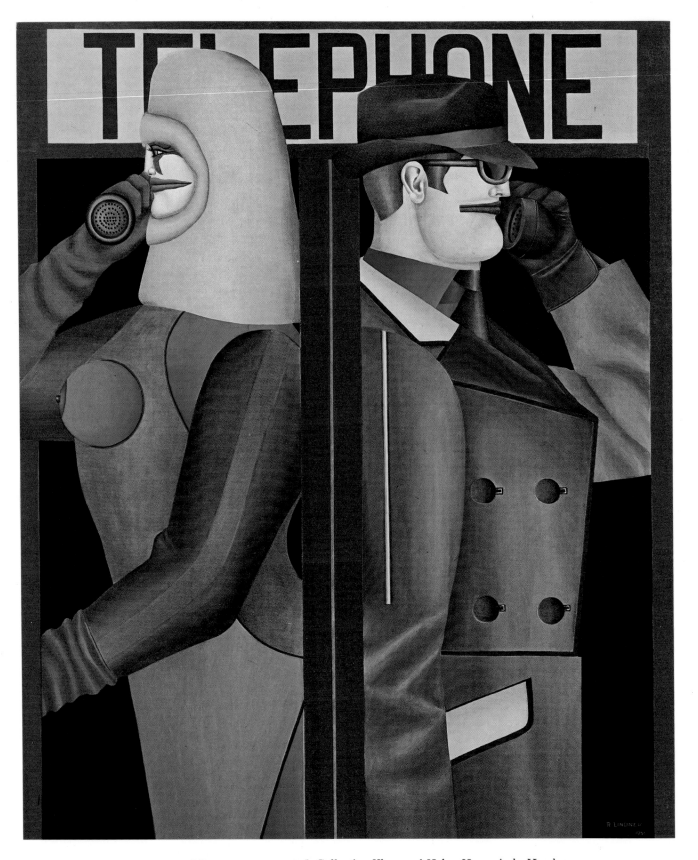

Plate 159. TELEPHONE. 1966. Oil on canvas, 70 × 60″. Collection Klaus and Helga Hegewisch, Hamburg

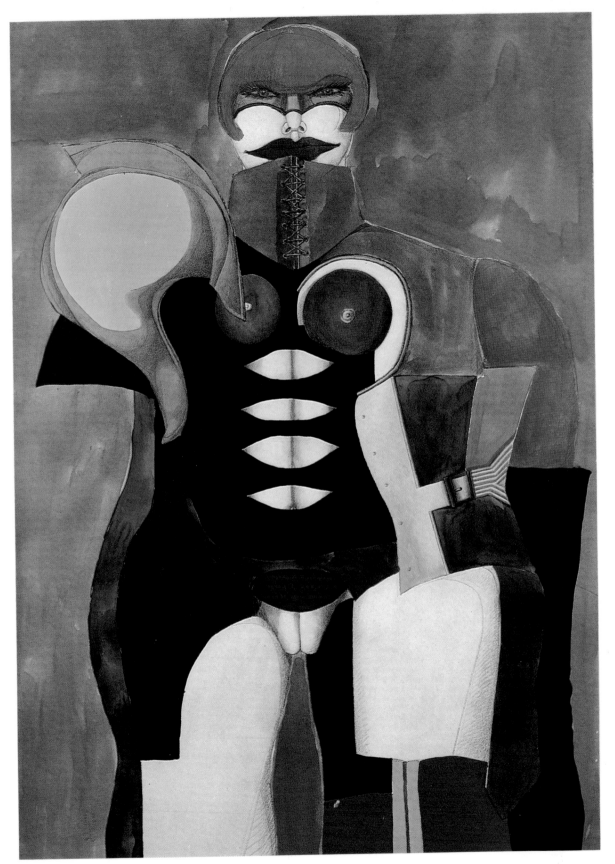

Plate 160.
ANGEL IN ME. 1966.
Watercolor, 39 1/8 × 28 5/8".
Collection Mr. and Mrs. Harris B. Steinberg,
New York

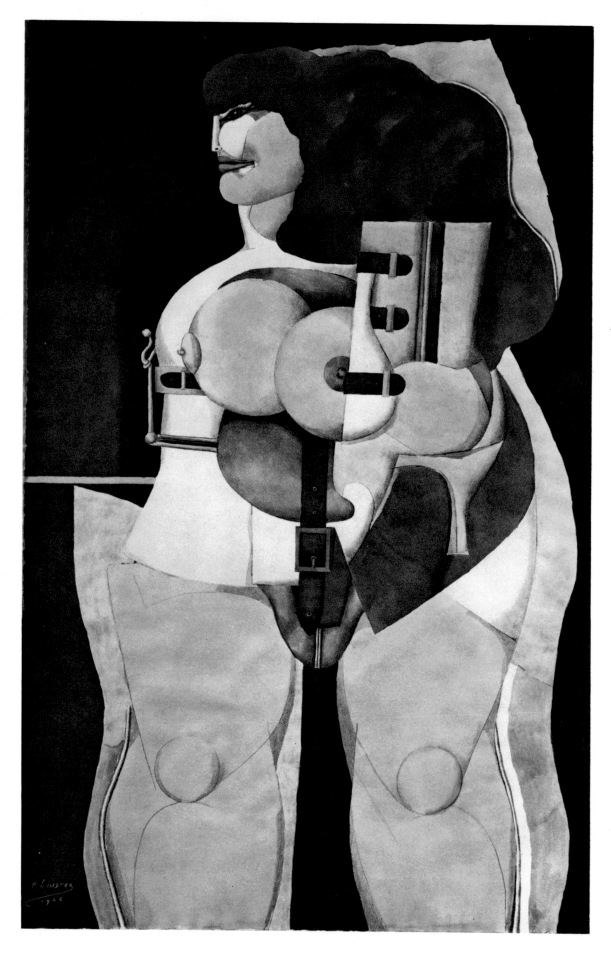

Plate 161.
Study for LEOPARD LILY. 1966.
Watercolor, 40 × 28 1/4″.
Collection Miss Helen Mary Harding,
New York

Plate 162. NO. 1966. Oil on canvas, 70×60″. Collection Mrs. Philip V. Harari, Johannesburg, South Africa

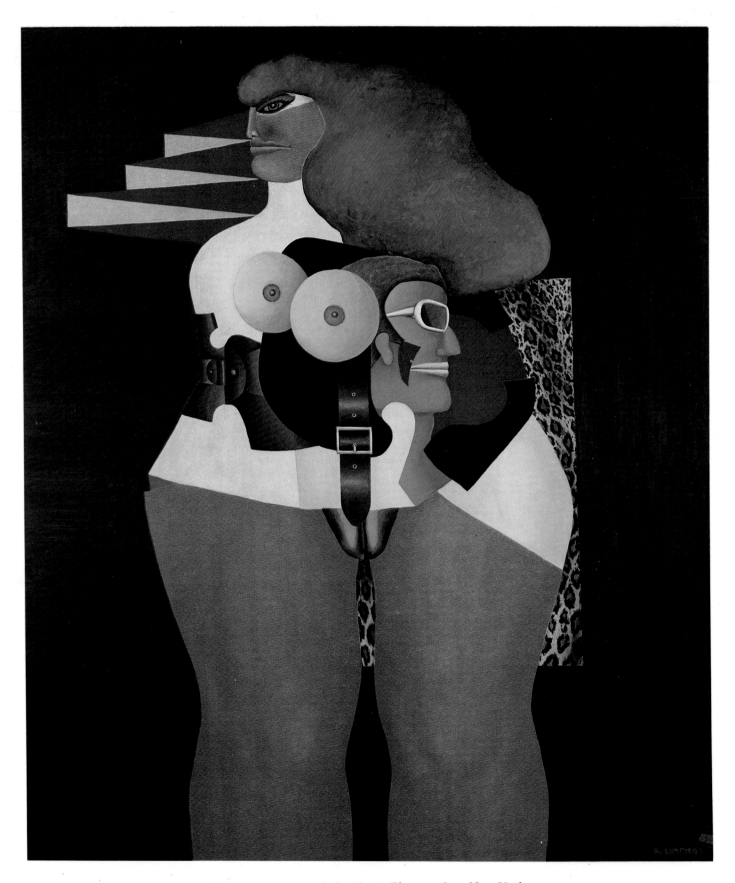

Plate 163. LEOPARD LILY. 1966. Oil on canvas, 70 × 60″. Cordier & Ekstrom, Inc., New York

Plate 164.
ANGEL IN ME.
1966. Oil on canvas, 70 × 60″.
Collection Mr. and Mrs. Robert B. Mayer,
Winnetka, Illinois

Plate 165. HEAD OF A WOMAN. 1966. Watercolor, 12 1/4 × 18 3/4″. The J. L. Hudson Gallery, Detroit, Michigan

Plate 166.
CHECKMATE. 1966.
Gouache, 23 7/8 × 18".
The Museum of Modern Art, New York

Plate 167. ICE. 1966. Oil on canvas, 70×60".
Whitney Museum of American Art, New York. Gift of the Friends of the Whitney Museum of American Art

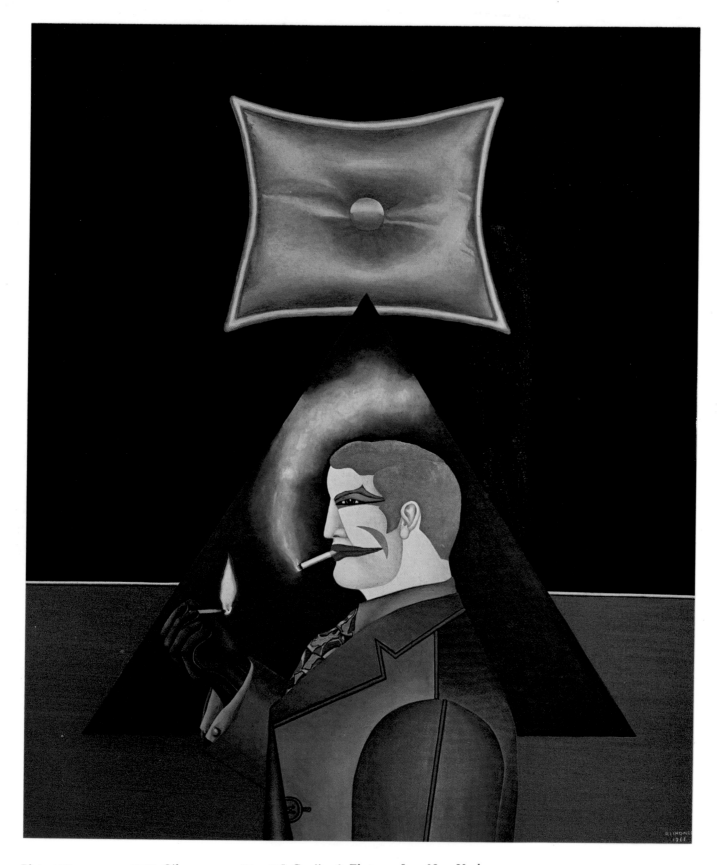

Plate 168. PILLOW. 1966. Oil on canvas, 70 × 60″. Cordier & Ekstrom, Inc., New York

Plate 169.
COUPLE. 1966.
Pencil, 20 × 17″.
Collection the artist

Plate 170.
ROCK-ROCK. 1966–67.
Oil on canvas, 70 × 60″.
Dallas Museum of Fine Arts,
Texas

Plate 171.
UNTITLED. 1967.
Watercolor, 24 3/4 × 18 5/8". Collection
Mr. and Mrs. Michael Calderon,
New York

Plate 172.
UNTITLED. 1967.
Watercolor, 40 × 28 1/4".
Collection Dr. and Mrs. Harry Y. Hoffman,
Detroit, Michigan

Plate 173.
UNTITLED. 1967.
Watercolor, 40 × 28 1/2".
Collection Jacques Kaplan,
New York

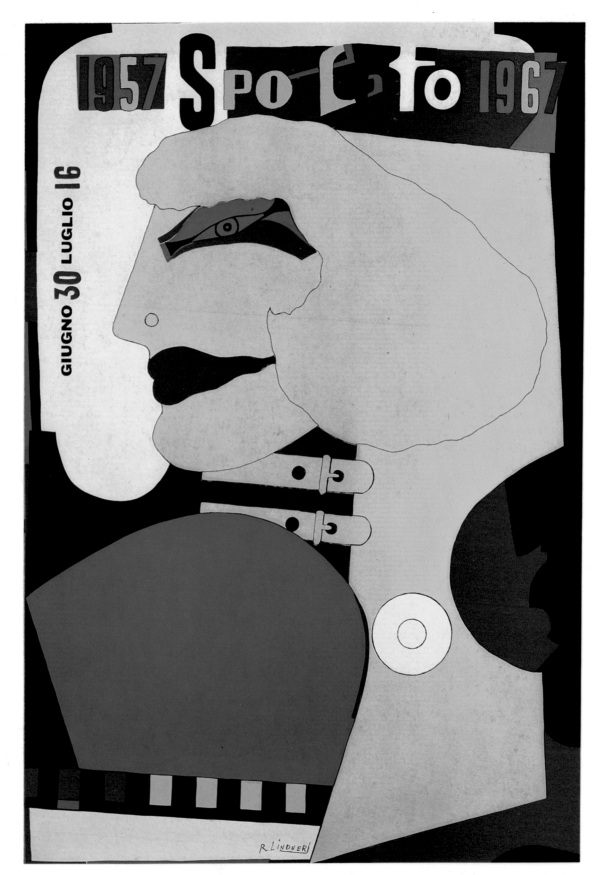

Plate 174.
SPOLETO. 1967.
Silkscreen poster, 40 × 27 1/8″

Plate 175.
ADULTS ONLY. 1967.
Watercolor, 40 × 20 3/4".
Cordier & Ekstrom, Inc., New York

Plate 176.
THANK YOU (WOMAN WITH PARROT). 1967.
Gouache, 41 1/2 × 30″.
Collection Clifford Grodd, Rye, New York

Plate 177.
MAN WITH PARROT. 1967.
Watercolor and collage, 40 × 27″.
Collection Mr. and Mrs. Richard L. Selle,
Chicago, Illinois

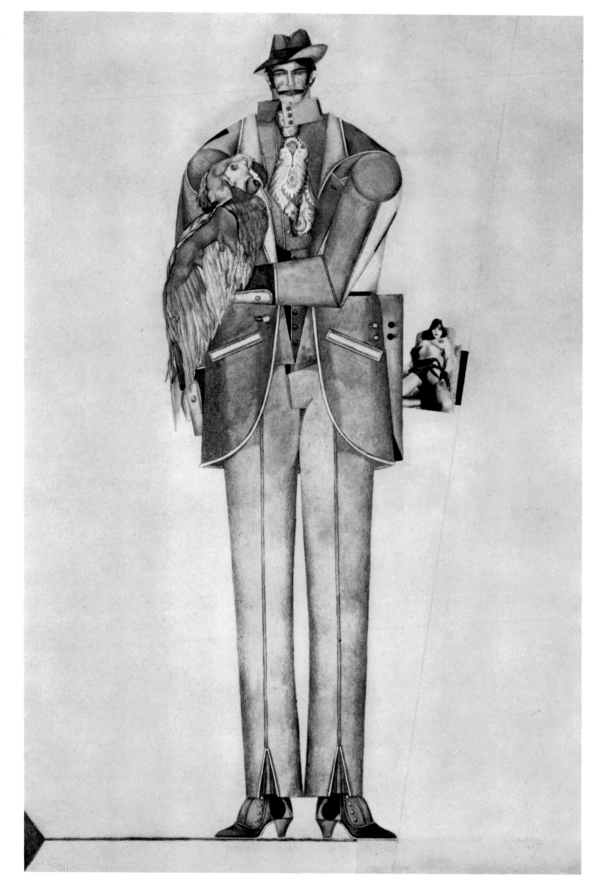

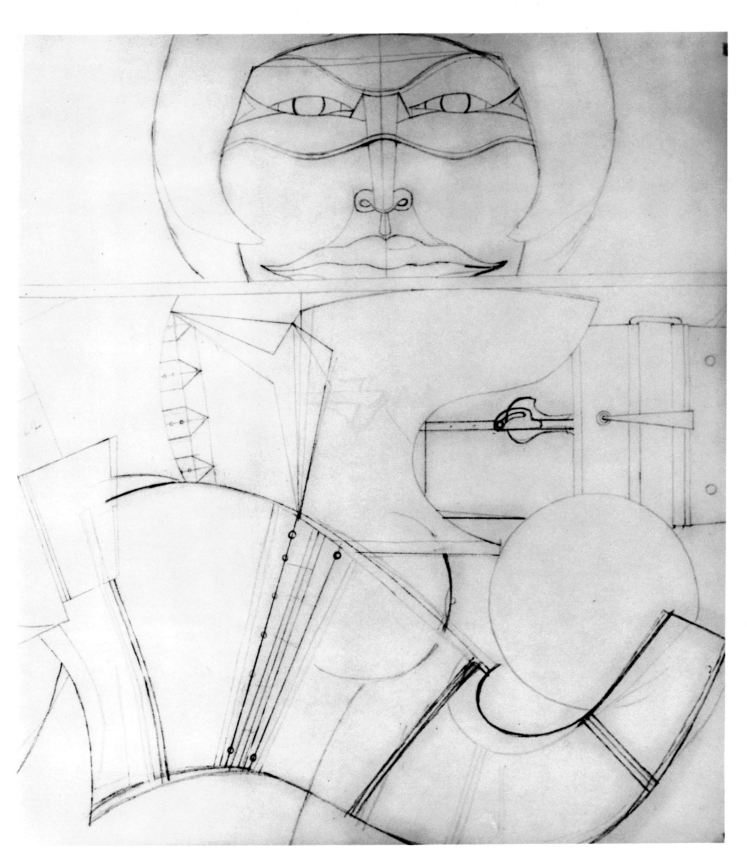

Plate 178.
UNTITLED. 1967.
Pencil, 32 × 28 1/2″.
Collection the artist

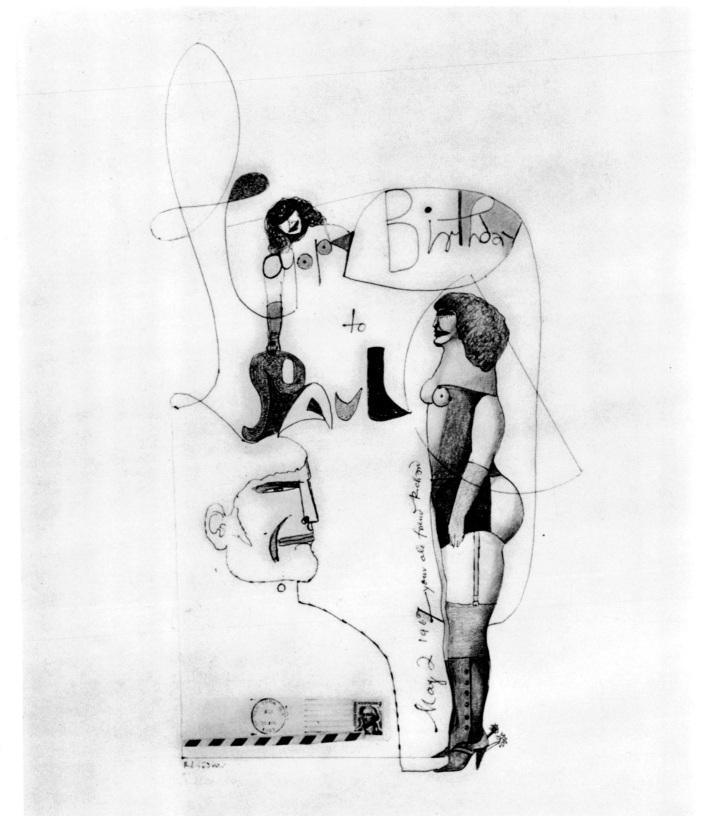

Plate 179.
HAPPY BIRTHDAY TO PAUL. 1967.
Pen, crayon, and collage, 22 × 18 1/2".
Collection Ingeborg Wiener-ten Haeff,
New York

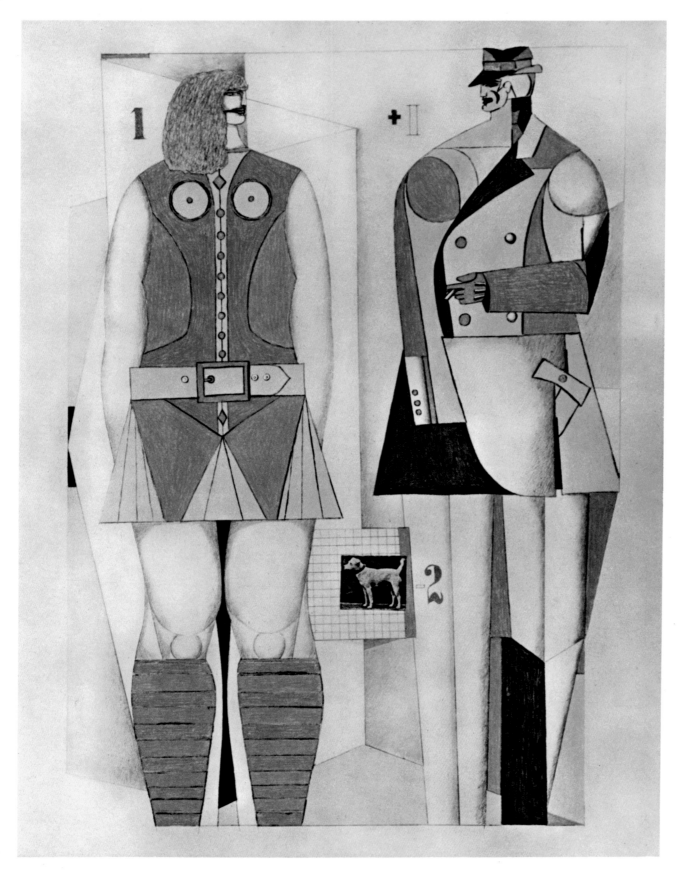

Plate 180.
1–2. 1967.
Silkscreen, 28 × 20″

Plate 181.
WE ARE ALL ONE. 1967.
Pencil and colored crayon,
23 3/4 × 18 3/4".
The J. L. Hudson Gallery,
Detroit, Michigan

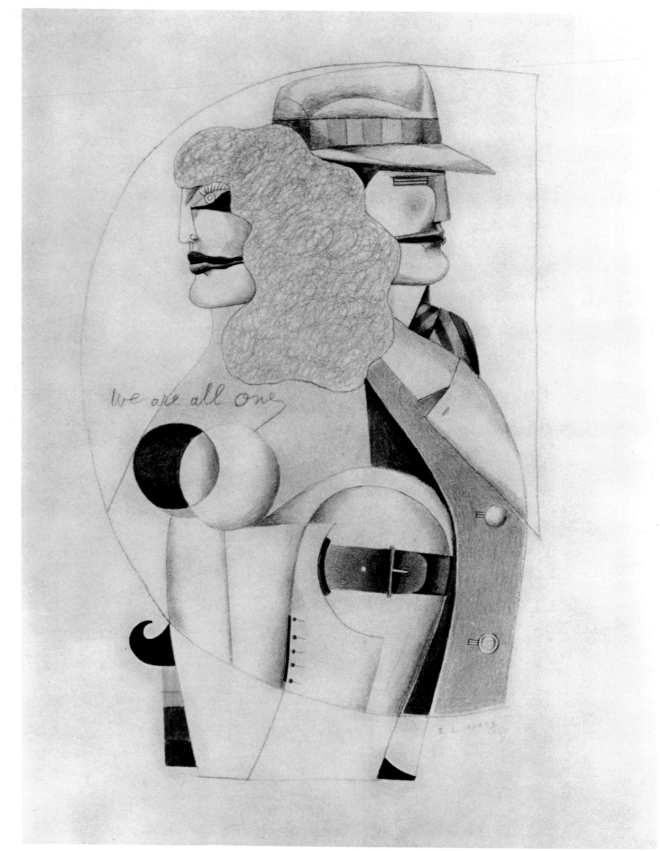

Plate 182. MARILYN WAS HERE. 1967. Watercolor and collage, 31 × 25 1/2″. Mr. and Mrs. Seymour M. Klein, New York

Plate 183.
MARILYN WAS HERE. 1967.
Oil on canvas, 72 × 60″.
Collection Dr. Max Palevsky,
Santa Monica, California

Plate 184.
WE ARE ALL ONE. 1967.
Lithograph, 22 × 16 1/2″

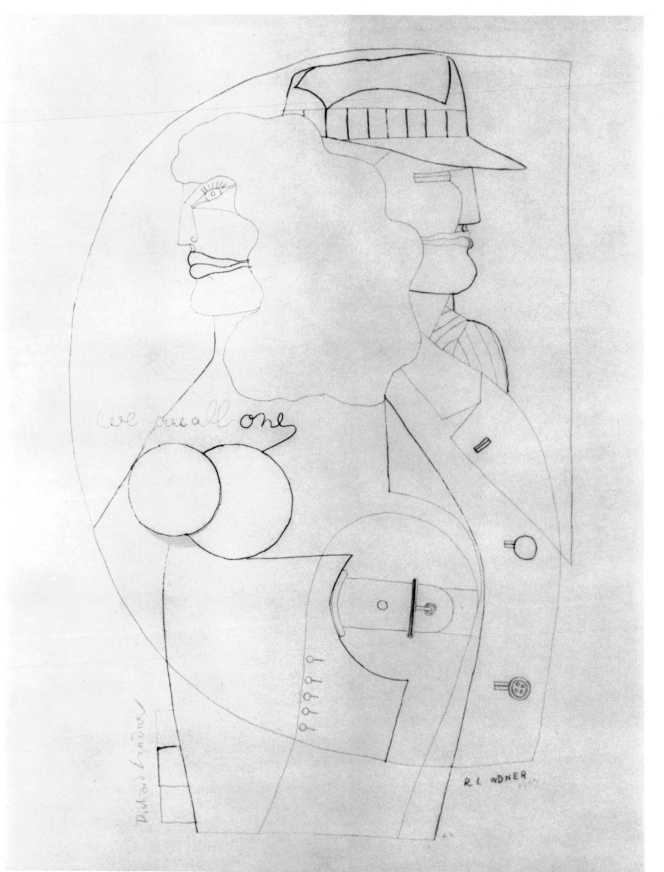

Plate 185.
"LENOX HILL HOSPITAL
AND SKOWHEGAN SCHOOL
OF PAINTING AND SCULPTURE."
1967. Silkscreen poster,
29 1/2 × 20 1/2"

Plate 186.
BANNER NO. 1. 1968.
Fabric, 84 × 48″.
Edition of 20. Courtesy Multiples, Inc.,
New York

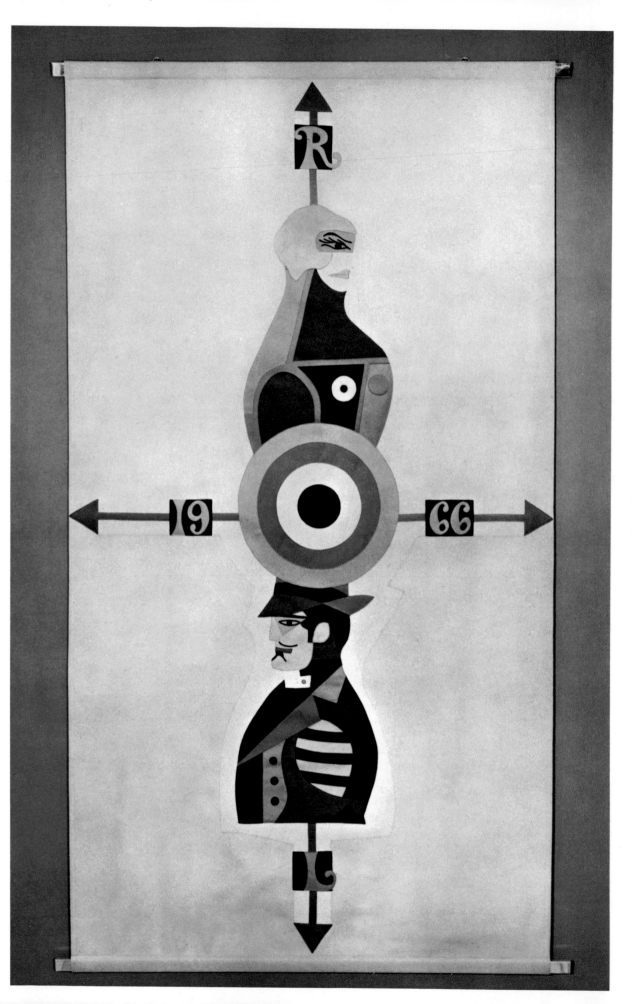

Plate 187.
BANNER NO. 2. 1968.
Fabric, 84×48″.
Edition of 20. Courtesy Multiples, Inc.,
New York

BIBLIOGRAPHY

1954

"First One Man Show in America at Betty Parsons Gallery," *Art News* (February, 1954), 44.

"Reviews and Previews," *Art News* (February, 1954). Signed B. G.

GENAUER, EMILY. "In the Art Galleries," *New York Herald Tribune* (January 31, 1954).

ROSENBLUM, ROBERT. "A Sophisticated Primitive; Exhibition at Betty Parsons Gallery," *Art Digest* (February 15, 1954), 13.

1956

"Exhibition of Paintings at Betty Parsons Gallery," *Art News* (February, 1956), 55. Signed E. C. M.

"Exhibition of Paintings and Drawings at Betty Parsons Gallery," *Arts* (March, 1956), 57. Signed A. V.

1959

ASHTON, DORE. "Art: Gallery Exhibitions," *New York Times* (February 26, 1959).

CAMPBELL, LAWRENCE. "Exhibition at Betty Parsons Gallery," *Art News* (February, 1959), 15.

GENAUER, EMILY. "Solo by Lindner," *New York Herald Tribune* (February 21, 1959).

PRESTON, STUART. "Shockers," *New York Times* (February 22, 1959).

1960

TILLIM, SIDNEY. *Lindner*. Chicago: William and Noma Copley Foundation, 1960.

1961

"Exhibition at Cordier-Warren," *Art News* (October, 1961), 10–11.

TILLIM, SIDNEY. "John Graham and Richard Lindner," *Arts* (November, 1961), 34–37.

1962

Art International (September, 1962), 37.

ASHTON, DORE. "Art U.S.A. 1962," *Studio* (March, 1962), 91.

———. "Exhibition at Cordier-Warren," *Arts and Architecture* (February, 1962), 6.

BUTCHER, GEORGE. "Striven Identity," *The Guardian* (July 11, 1962), 5.

MELVILLE, R. "First London Exhibition," *The Architectural Review* (November, 1962), 363.

"Mr. Lindner's Paintings," *The Times of London* (June 25, 1962).

REICHARDT, J. "Les Expositions à L'Etranger: Londres," *Aujourd'hui* (September, 1962), 58.

ROBERTS, COLETTE. "Lettre de New York," *Aujourd'hui* (September, 1962), 61.

SANDLER, IRVING. "In the Art Galleries," *New York Post* (June 17, 1962).

TILLIM, SIDNEY. "Richard Lindner," *Aujourd'hui* (February, 1962), 26–29.

WHITTET, G. S. *Studio* (September, 1962), 116.

1963

ASHTON, DORE. "Americans at the Museum of Modern Art," *Arts and Architecture* (July, 1963), 4.

BARO, G. "Gathering of Americans," *Arts* (September, 1963), 33.

HESS, THOMAS B. "Phony Crisis in American Art," *Art News* (Summer, 1963), 28.

LANGSNER, JULES. "Los Angeles Letter," *Art International* (June, 1963), 77.

LINDNER, RICHARD. "Statement," *Americans 1963*, Museum of Modern Art publication.

SECKLER, DOROTHY G. "The Artist in America: Victim of the Cultural Boom?" *Art in America* (December, 1963), 28–39.

1964

ASHTON, DORE. "Die Zeichnung in der modernen amerikanischen Kunst, I." *Internationale der Zeichnung*, Darmstadt (November, 1964), 29–43.

————. "Richard Lindner: The Secret of the Inner Voice," *Studio* (January, 1964), 12–17.

"Exhibition at Cordier-Ekstrom," *Art News* (March, 1964), 10. Signed S. G.

KELLY, E. T. "Neo-Dada: A Critique of Pop Art," *Art Journal* (Spring, 1964), 200.

MONTE, JAMES. "Americans 1963, San Francisco Museum of Art," *Art Forum* (September, 1964), 43–44.

O'DOHERTY, BRIAN. "Lindner's Private but Very Modern Hades," *New York Times* (March 8, 1964).

"Painter of the Crass Crowd," *Time Magazine* (March 20, 1964), 70.

RAYNOR, VIVIAN. "Exhibition at Cordier-Ekstrom," *Arts* (May, 1964), 41.

ROBERTS, COLETTE. "Les Expositions à New York," *Aujourd'hui* (January, 1964), 96.

"Stop, Caution, Go," *Newsweek* (March 9, 1964), 53.

WILLARD, CHARLOTTE. "Drawing Today," *Art in America* (October, 1964), 64.

1965

DIENST, ROLF-GUNTER. "Richard Lindner," *Das Kunstwerk* (August, 1965), 21.

"Collages and Paintings at Cordier-Ekstrom," *Art News* (April, 1965), 11. Signed N.E.

"Exhibition at Cordier-Ekstrom," *Time Magazine* (February 26, 1965).

"Flags, New Glories," *Time Magazine* (April 9, 1965).

FRIGERIO. "Exposition à la Galerie Claude Bernard," *Aujourd'hui* (July, 1965), 87.

GRUEN, JOHN. "Three 'Old Masters,'" *New York Herald Tribune* (February, 1965), 28.

LEVÊQUE, JEAN-JACQUES. "Richard Lindner," *La Nouvelle Revue Française* (October, 1965), 735–36.

LINDNER, RICHARD. "Statement," *Art Voices* (Fall, 1965), 64.

PRESTON, STUART. "Art: Hans Hofmann at a Vigorous 85," *New York Times* (February 20, 1965), 22.

ROSENTHAL, N. "Six Day Bicycle Wheel Race: Multiple Originals," *Art in America* (October, 1965), 101.

SCHULZ, FRANZ. "The Corcoran's American Mixture, 1965," *New York Times* (February 28, 1965).

STILES, G. "Exhibition at Cordier-Ekstrom," *Arts* (April, 1965), 65.

1966

"Eros in Polyester," *Newsweek* (October 10, 1966).

GRUEN, JOHN. "The Art of Cruelty," New York *World Journal Tribune, New York Magazine* (October, 1966).

HENNING, E. B. "German Expressionist Paintings at the Cleveland Museum of Art," *Burlington Magazine* (December, 1966), 632–33.

"Portrait," *Das Kunstwerk*, (April, 1966), 109.

1967

"Artists: Baal Booster," *Time Magazine* (February 3, 1967), 44.

ASHTON, DORE. "Exhibition at Cordier-Ekstrom," *Arts and Architecture* (March, 1967), 4.

———. "Exhibition at Cordier-Ekstrom," *Studio* (March, 1967), 153.

———. "New York Gallery Notes: Show at Cordier-Ekstrom," *Art in America* (January, 1967), 90.

"Ausstellung in New York," *Kunstwerk* (February, 1967), 22–26.

GLUECK, GRACE. "Art Notes: Macy's Is His Louvre," *New York Times* (January 15, 1967).

GRUEN, JOHN. "Richard Lindner's Nightmare Women," *New York World Journal Tribune* (January 15, 1967), 26–27.

KRAMER, HILTON. "Richard Lindner: 'A Dream of Decadent Vitality,'" *New York Times* (January 22, 1967), 25.

PENROSE, ROLAND, "Richard Lindner," *Art International* (January 20, 1967), 30–32.

PERREAULT, JOHN. "Venus in Vinyl," *Art News* (January, 1967), 46–48.

PICARD, LIL. "The Turn of the Brush," *East Village Other* (January 15–February 1, 1967), 14.